CONTE

CW00558641

0860 10 50 50
www.mapstudio.co.za

Production Manager: John Loubser
Cartography: Rudi de Lange

Due to the dynamic nature of name changes both at street level and nationally we recognise the importance of keeping you, our map users as up-to-date as possible. Name changes are implemented in our products at the time of compilation , only once they have been made official. Should any other name changes be registered too late to be reflected in any of our products we will list them on our website - www.mapstudio.co.za . These are available as free downloads for your convenience and can be obtained under our "downloads & links" section. It is our goal to keep our list of name changes on our website as current as possible– please note however that it will only list official name changes and not proposed ones.

The publishers acknowledge with thanks the great assistance of Municipal and Local Authorities, and various Government Departments on whom the information largely depends, in the revision of the Atlas. Every reasonable care has been taken to ensure that the information in this book is correct at the time of compilation. Nevertheless, the publishers can accept no responsibility for errors or omissions, nor for change of details given. Compiled and produced by Map Studio. Company Reg. no. 1991/001851/07.

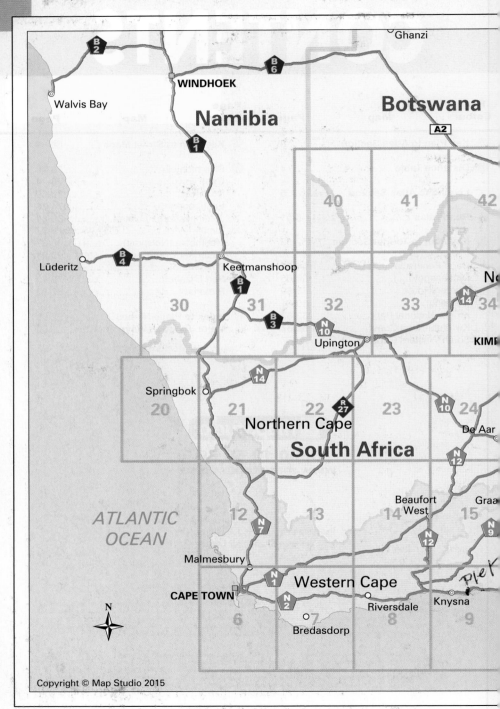

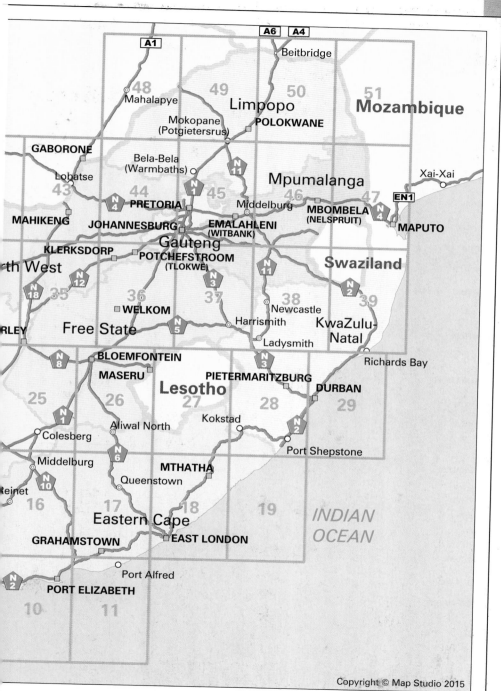

	PRETORIA	PORT ELIZABETH	MTHATHA	MBABANE	MASERU	MAPUTO	MAHIKENG	KIMBERLEY	JOHANNESBURG	GABORONE	EAST LONDON	DURBAN	CAPE TOWN	BLOEMFONTEIN
BLOEMFONTEIN	455	681	570	677	157	862	464	177	398	622	584	634	1004	•
CAPE TOWN	1460	769	1314	1680	1160	1865	1343	969	1402	1501	1079	1753	•	1004
COLESBERG	682	451	517	903	383	1085	672	292	624	848	488	860	778	226
DURBAN	636	984	439	562	590	620	821	811	557	979	674	•	1753	634
EAST LONDON	1040	310	235	1238	630	1301	1048	780	982	1206	•	674	1079	584
GABORONE	350	1299	1192	719	702	919	158	538	358	•	1206	979	1501	622
GEORGE	1229	335	880	1450	913	1670	1203	762	1171	1361	645	1319	438	773
GRAAFF-REINET	880	291	503	1101	599	1283	854	490	822	1012	395	942	787	424
GRAHAMSTOWN	1057	130	415	1418	692	1478	1065	667	999	1223	180	854	899	601
JOHANNESBURG	58	1075	869	361	438	555	287	476	•	358	982	557	1402	398
KEETMANSHOOP	1354	1429	1547	1657	1283	1851	1072	897	1296	1230	1468	1708	995	1074
KIMBERLEY	530	743	747	833	334	1033	380	•	476	538	780	811	962	177
LADYSMITH	414	1062	517	386	366	529	597	587	356	755	752	248	1413	410
MBOMBELA (NELSPRUIT)	322	1434	976	173	713	206	635	827	355	672	1226	707	1762	757
MAHIKENG	294	1141	1034	648	544	848	•	380	287	158	1048	821	1343	464
MAPUTO	545	1609	1064	223	815	•	848	1033	555	919	1301	620	1865	862
MASERU	488	822	616	633	•	815	544	334	438	702	630	590	1160	157
MBABANE	372	1548	1003	•	633	223	648	833	361	719	1238	562	1680	677
MTHATHA	928	545	•	1003	616	1064	1034	747	869	1192	235	439	1314	570
MUSINA	447	1594	1392	797	949	687	680	991	505	696	1501	1107	1921	928
PIETERMARITZBURG	557	905	360	640	511	706	742	732	499	900	595	79	1664	555
POLOKWANE	250	1383	1181	504	738	567	569	780	297	485	1290	886	1710	706
PORT ELIZABETH	1133	•	545	1548	822	1609	1141	743	1075	1299	310	984	769	681
PRETORIA	•	1133	928	372	488	545	294	530	58	350	1040	636	1460	455
UPINGTON	854	933	1047	1157	731	1357	572	397	796	730	968	1208	894	574
WELKOM	316	830	718	451	249	775	321	294	258	479	737	564	1156	153

Although the greatest care has been taken in compiling the kilometre table and ensuring that the road distances given conform to the latest information available, no responsibility for errors can be accepted by the publishers, who would welcome any suggested amendments. The kilometres indicate the shortest distance between any two places over tarred roads wherever possible.

To find the distance between any two places in the table read down and across the respective connecting columns. An example is given above in which the distance between Cape Town and Pretoria is shown as 1460 kilometres.

Copyright © Map Studio 2015

Tarred ▬▬▬▬ Untarred	Freeway / National Road
Under Construction	Main Road
	Secondary Road
N1 R21 R110	Route Numbers
Ⓣ Ⓣ	Toll Route and Toll Plaza
	Mountain Pass
15	Distance in Kilometres
●━━	Railway and Station
	International Boundary / Provincial Boundary
	Water Feature
	Marsh / Pan
	National Park and Nature Reserve
▢	Capital or City
◎	Major Town
○	Secondary Town
⊙	Other Town
○	Settlement
🏠	Accommodation
♟	Historical Site
◀	Border Control
✈	Major Airport
✛	Airfield
▲	Major Spot Height
▲	Place of Interest
═	Waterfall
⚔	Battlefield

MAJOR JUNCTION WAYPOINTS (GPS POINTS)

The point of the arrow indicates the waypoint for this particular junction and its accompanying label. The junction is given a unique label and a list of these labels with their corresponding co-ordinates can be found on page 100.

J28

0 5 10   20   30   40   50km

Scale 1 : 1 500 000

Scale 1 : 1 500 00

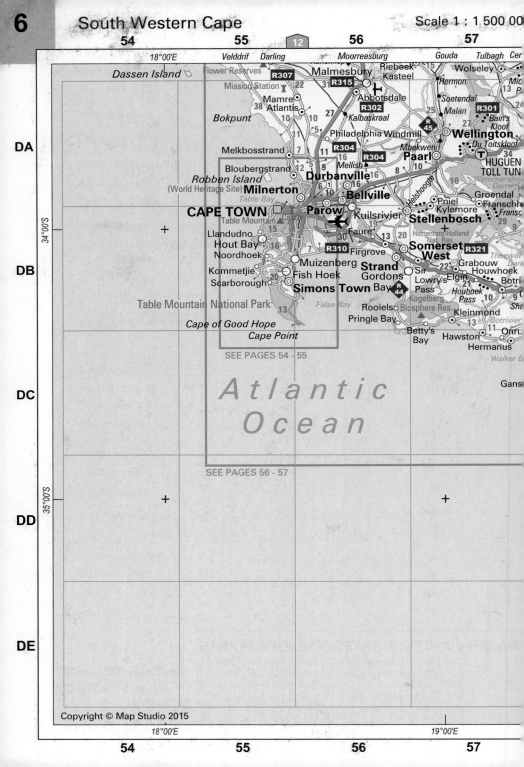

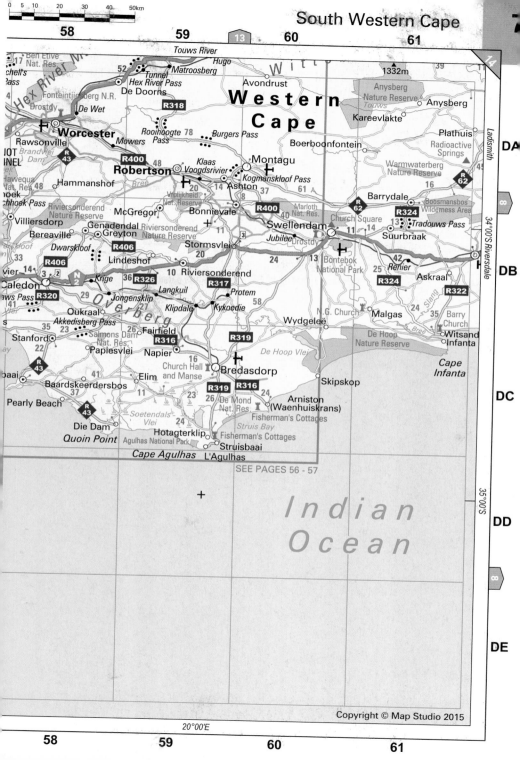

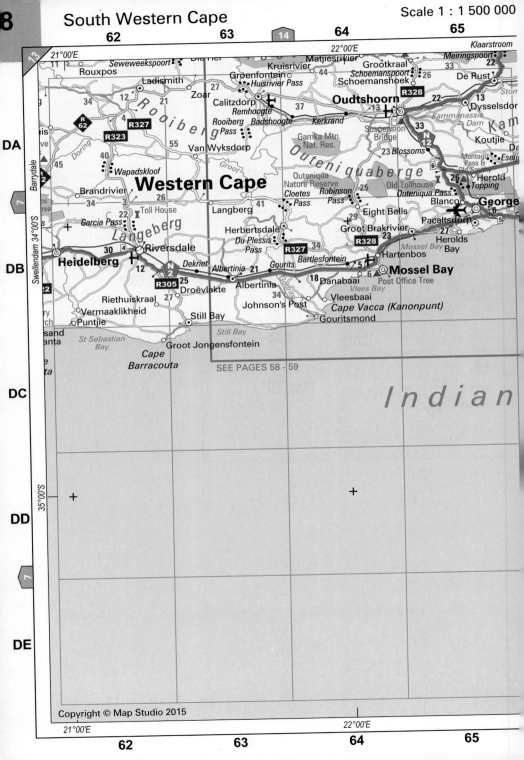

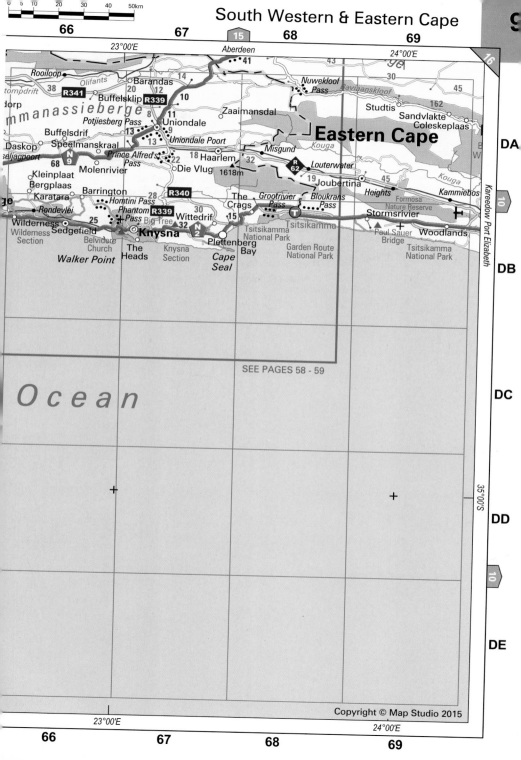

0 5 10   20   30   40   50km

66   67   **15**   68   69

23°00'E   Aberdeen   24°00'E   16

Rooiloop
Olifants   41
Barandas   14   43   Nuwekloof   30
38   R341   Buffelsklip R339   20   12   Pass   Saviaansloof   45
Horp   mmanassieberge   8   10   Studtis   162
Potjiesberg Pass   11   Zaaimansdal   Sandvlakte
Buffelsdrif   13   9   Uniondale   Coleskeplaas
Speelmanskraal   13   **Eastern Cape**
Daskop   N9   Uniondale Poort   Kouga   DA
seljagpoort   68   Prince Alfred's   18 Haarlem   Misgund   B
Kleinplaat   Pass   22   32   R   Louterwater   W   10
Bergplaas   Molenrivier   Die Vlug   1618m   62   Kouga
Karatara   Barrington   28   R340   19 Joubertina   45
e   Rondevlei   Homtini Pass   The   Grootrivier   Bloukrans   Heights   Kammiebos
25   Phantom R339   Crags   Pass   Pass   Formosa   Woodlands
Wilderness   Pass Big Tree   30   Wittedrif   15   Tsitsikamma   Nature Reserve   DB
Wilderness   Sedgefield   32   N2   Stormsrivier
Section   Belvidere   The   Knysna   Plettenberg   Tsitsikamma   Paul Sauer
Church   Heads   Section   Bay   National Park   Bridge   Tsitsikamma
Walker Point   Cape   Garden Route   National Park
Seal   National Park

SEE PAGES 58 - 59

Ocean

Kareedow Port Elizabeth

DC

35°00'S

+   +   DD

10

DE

Copyright © Map Studio 2015

23°00'E   24°00'E

66   67   68   69

Scale 1 : 1 500 000

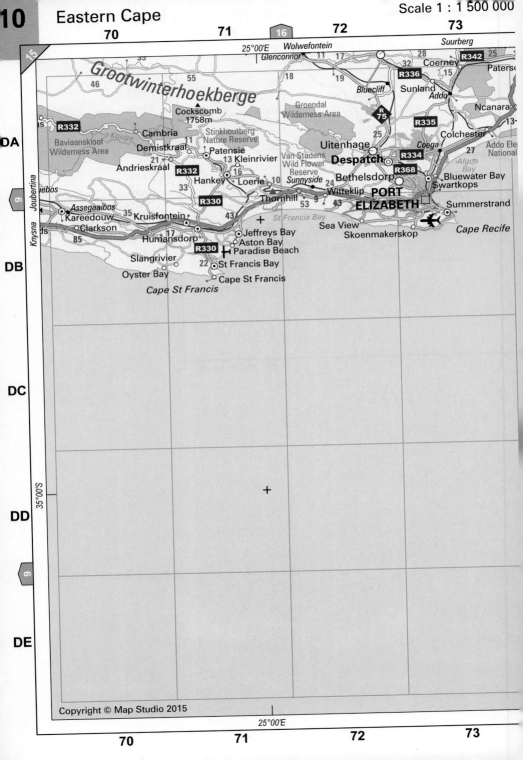

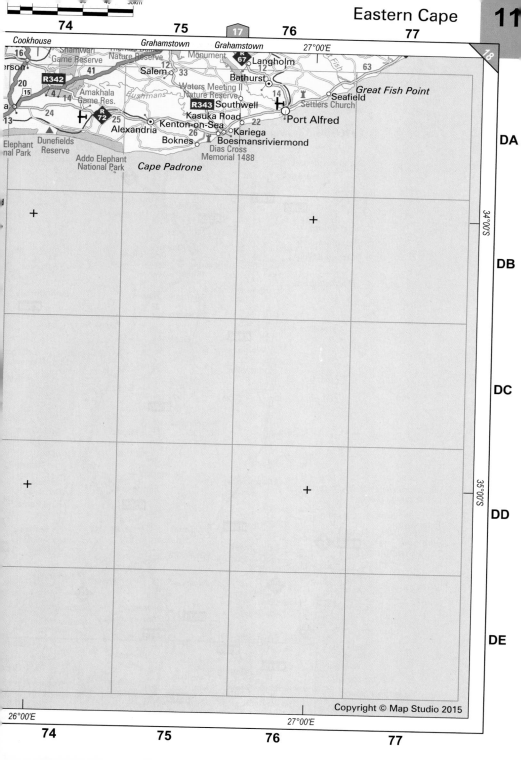

74　　　　75　　17　　76　　77

Cookhouse　　　Grahamstown　Grahamstown

27°00'E

18

Shamwari
Game Reserve

Thomas Baines
Nature Reserve

Grahamstown
Monument

67 Langholm

erson

16

Salem　33　12

Bathurst

63

41

R342

20

15

4

14

Amakhala
Game Res.

14

Bushmans

Waters Meeting II
Nature Reserve

Southwell
R343

14

Seafield
Settlers Church

Great Fish Point

24

R
72

25

Kasuka Road

22

Port Alfred

13

Alexandria

Kenton-on-Sea

26

Kariega

Boesmansriviermond

Elephant
nal Park

Dunefields
Reserve

Boknes

Dias Cross
Memorial 1488

Addo Elephant
National Park

Cape Padrone

DA

34°00'S

+　　　　　+

DB

35°00'S

DC

+　　　　　+

DD

DE

26°00'E

27°00'E

74　　　　75　　76　　77

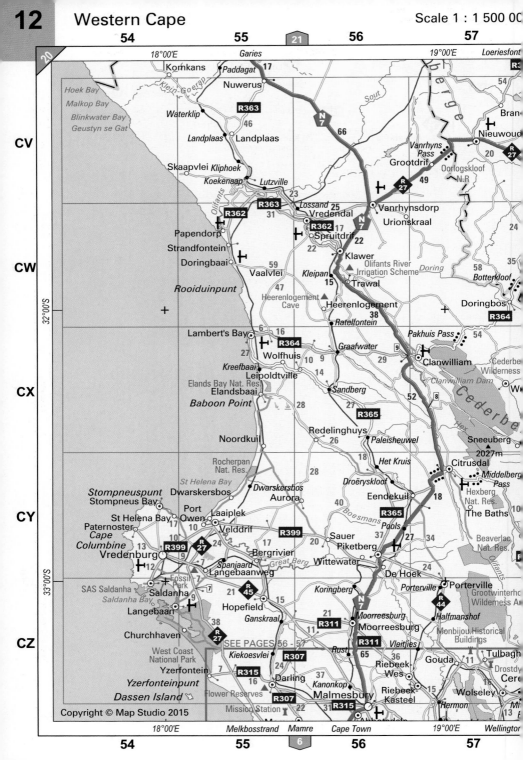

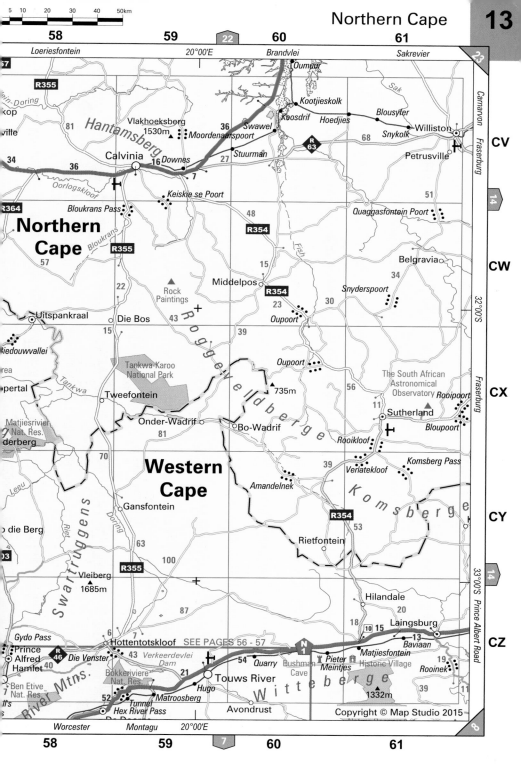

5 10 20 30 40 50km

| 58 | 59 | 22 | 60 | 61 | 23 |

Loeriesfontein · 20°00'E · Brandvlei · Sakrevier

Carnarvon Fraserburg

CV

R355

ein-Doring
kop

Oumuur

Kootjieskolk

Blousyfer

Koosdrif · Hoedjies

81 · Hantamsberg · Vlakhoeksberg 1530m · 36 · Swawel · Snykolk · Williston

ville · Moordenaarspoort · 68

34 · Calvinia · 16 · Downes · 27 · Stuurman · Petrusville

36 · 7

Oorlogskloof

Keiskie se Poort

CW

R364 · Bloukrans Pass · 48 · Quaggasfontein Poort · 51

Northern Cape · R354

57 · R355 · 15 · Belgravia

22 · Middelpos · R354 · 34

Rock Paintings · Snyderspoort

Uitspankraal · Die Bos · 43 · 23 · 30

15 · 39 · Oupoort

iedouwvallei

Oupoort

CX

rea · Tankwa-Karoo National Park · The South African Astronomical Observatory · Rooipoort

pertal · Tankwa · 735m · 56 · 11

Tweefontein · Sutherland

Matjiesrivier Nat. Res. · Onder-Wadrif · Bo-Wadrif · Bloupoort

derberg · 81 · Rooikloof

70 · 39 · Komsberg Pass

Western Cape · Verlatekloof

Leeu · Amandelnek · Komsberg

Gansfontein · R354

CY

o die Berg · 63 · 53

03 · Riet · Doring · 100 · Rietfontein

Vleiberg 1685m · R355

87 · Hilandale

CZ

20 · 18 · 10 · 15 · Laingsburg

Gydo Pass · 6 · 7 · Hottentotskloof · SEE PAGES 56 - 57 · 13 · Baviaan

Prince Alfred Hamlet · 46 · Die Venster · 43 · Verkeerdevlei Dam · 21 · 54 · Quarry · Pieter Meintjes · Matjiesfontein Historic Village · 19 · Rooinek

40 · Bokkeriviere Nat. Res. · Bushman Cave · 1332m · 39 · 11

Ben Etive Nat. Res. · Hugo · Touws River · Witteberge

it's · 52 · Tunnel · Matroosberg · Avondrust

Hex River Pass · Copyright © Map Studio 2015

River Mtns.

Worcester · Montagu · 20°00'E

| 58 | 59 | 7 | 60 | 61 |

Prince Albert Road

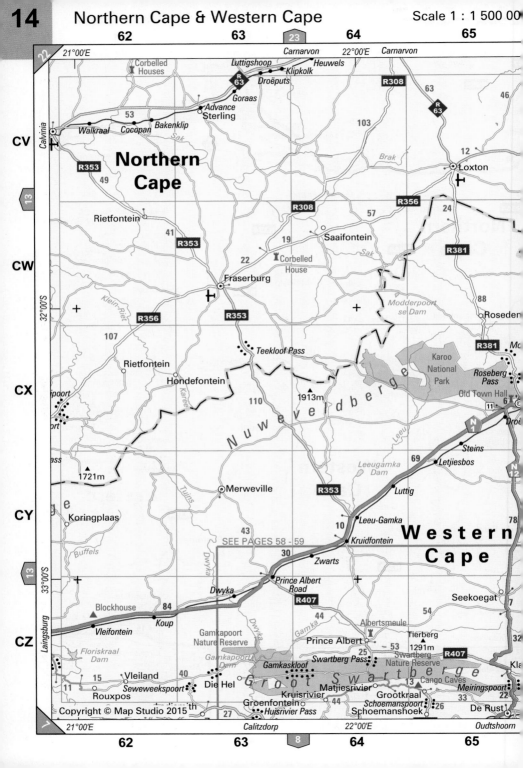

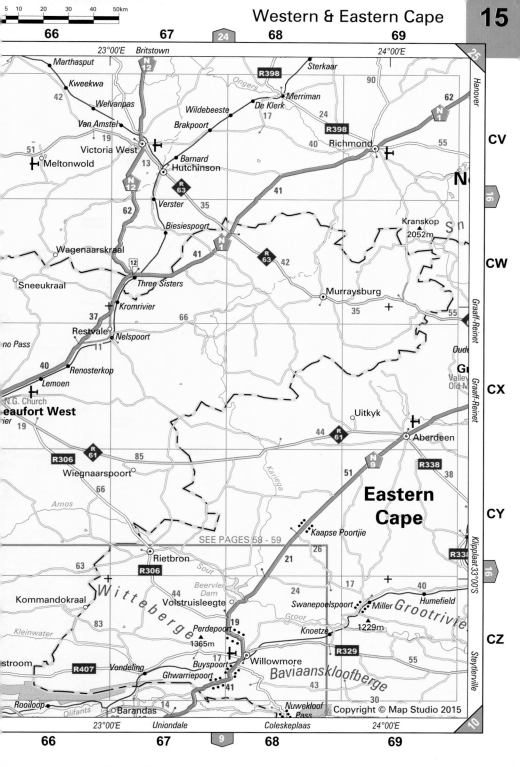

5 10 20 30 40 50km

66 67 24 68 69

23°00'E Britstown 24°00'E

Marthasput
Kweekwa
Welvanpas
42
Van Amstel
19
51
Victoria West
Meltonwold
13
Barnard
Hutchinson
N12
62
Verster 35
Biesiespoort
Wagenaarskraal
12
41
41
Sneeukraal
Three Sisters
42
Kromrivier
37
66
Restvale
11
Nelspoort
40
Renosterkop
Lemoen
N.G. Church
eaufort West
ier
19
R306
R61
85
Wiegnaarspoort
66
Amos
SEE PAGES 58 - 59
Rietbron
63
R306
Sout
Kommandokraal
Witteberge
44
Volstruisleegte
83
Perdepoort
1365m
Kleinwater
17
stroom
R407
Vondeling
Buyspoort
Ghwarriepoort
41
Rooiloop
Olifants
14
Barandas
23°00'E Uniondale

R398
Sterkaar
Merriman
90
De Klerk
Wildebeeste
17
24
Brakpoort
R398
Richmond
40
55
N12
41
Kranskop
2052m
Sn
R63
N1
R63
Murraysburg
35
55
Oude
Uitkyk
44
R61
Aberdeen
N9
R338
51
38
Eastern
Cape
Kaapse Poortjie
R33
26
21
R33
24
17
40
Humefield
Swanepoelspoort
Miller
Grootrivie
Knoetze
1229m
19
R329
55
Willowmore
Baviaanskloofberge
43
30
Nuwekloof
Pass
Coleskeplaas 24°00'E

Hanover
25
N1
62
N1
16
Graaff-Reinet
Graaff-Reinet
Klipplaat
16
Steytlerville
10

N

CV

CW

CX

CY

CZ

33°00'S

Copyright © Map Studio 2015

66 67 9 68 69

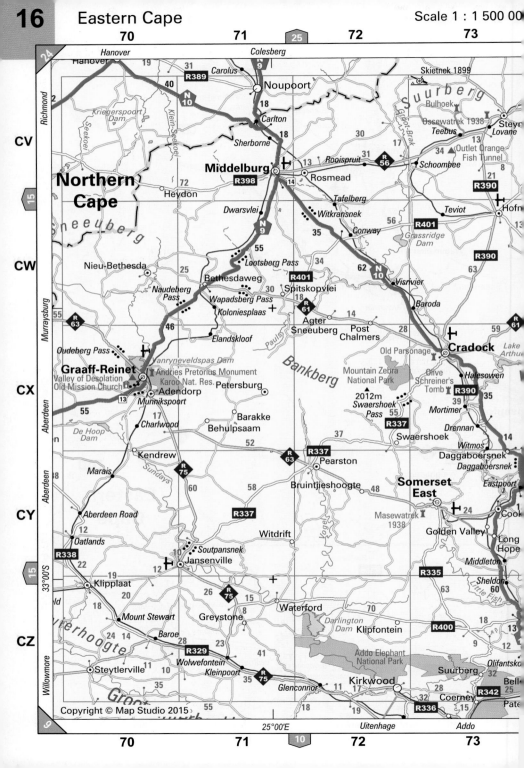

70   **71**   25   **72**   **73**

24

CV

CW

CX

CY

CZ

15

15

Richmond

Hanover
Hanover
19
31
R389
40
Carolus
Noupoort
N10
N9
18
Colesberg
Skietnek 1899
Carlton
18
Sherborne
30
Middelburg
R398
13
Rosmead
14
Rooispruit
R56
31
17
34
Schoombee
Teebus
Lovane
Steyn
Ossewatrek 1938
Bulhoek
SUURBERG
Groot-Brak
13
21
Outlet Orange-
Fish Tunnel
Hofn

Northern Cape

Heydon
72
Sneeuberg
Murraysburg
55
R63
Nieu-Bethesda
25
Naudeberg Pass
Dwarsvlei
N9
55
Lootsberg Pass
34
Bethesdaweg
R401
Wapadsberg Pass
30
Spitskopvlei
18
R61
Koloniesplaas
14
Agter Sneeuberg
Post Chalmers
28
Witkransnek
35
Conway
Tafelberg
56
R401
62
N10
Visrivier
Baroda
Grassridge Dam
63
R390
R390
Teviot
R61
59

Aberdeen

Oudeberg Pass
Graaff-Reinet
Valley of Desolation
Old Mission Church
Vanryneveldspas Dam
Andries Pretorius Monument
Karoo Nat. Res.
Petersburg
46
Elandskloof
Pauls
Bankberg
Mountain Zebra National Park
Old Parsonage
Olive Schreiner's Tomb
Cradock
Lake Arthur
2012m
Swaershoek Pass
55
R337
Halesowen
39
Mortimer
R390
35
13
Adendorp
Munnikspoort
55
17
Charlwood
Barakke
Behulpsaam
52
37
Swaershoek
Drennan
Witmos
14
Daggaboersnek
Daggaboersnek
Kendrew
R63
R337
Pearston
58
Bruintjieshoogte
48
Somerset East
Eastpoort
60
75
Marais
De Hoop Dam
Sundays
Aberdeen
Aberdeen Road
12
Oatlands
R337
Witdrift
Masewatrek 1938
24
Golden Valley
Cook
Long Hope
Middleton
Sheldon
Little Fish
R338
22
19
Klipplaat
20
18
10
12
Soutpansnek
Jansenville
+
Vogel
70
R335
63
60
Mount Stewart
24
14
Baroe
28
26
75
15
Greystone
8
Waterford
Darlington Dam
Klipfontein
18
R400
13
12
Steytlerville
11
10
R329
Wolwefontein
Kleinpoort
23
41
35
75
Glenconnor
11
17
Kirkwood
Suurberg
Olifantsko
32
28
Coerney
R342
25
Bell
Pate
R336
19
18
Addo Elephant National Park
Groot
35
55
Uitterhoogte
Willowmore
Groot

25°00'E
Uitenhage
Addo

33°00'S

Kriegerspoort Dam

Seekoei

Klein-Seekoei

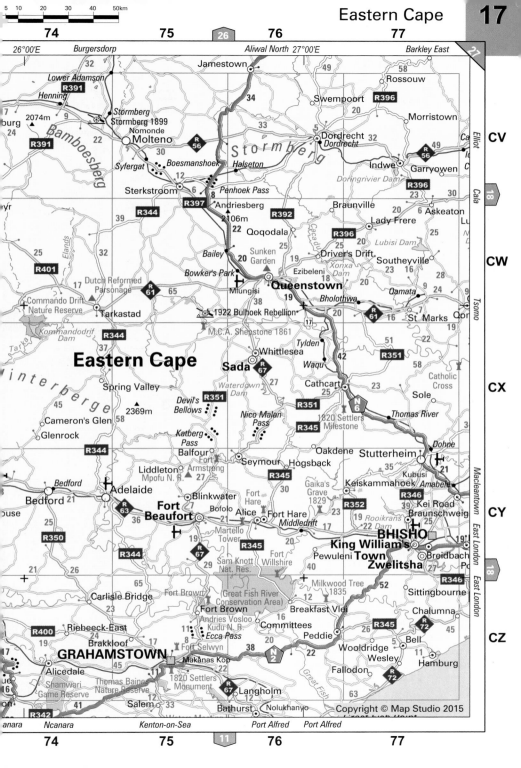

Map of Eastern Cape region showing places including Burgersdorp, Aliwal North, Barkley East, Jamestown, Rossouw, Lower Adamson, Henning, Swempoort, Morristown, Stormberg, Nomonde, Molteno, Dordrecht, Syfergat, Boesmanshoek, Halseton, Indwe, Garryowen, Sterkstroom, Penhoek Pass, Andriesberg, Braunville, Askeaton, Lady Frere, Qoqodala, Bailey, Sunken Garden, Driver's Drift, Southeyville, Bowker's Park, Ezibeleni, Qamata, Dutch Reformed Parsonage, Mlungisi, Queenstown, Bholothwa, St Marks, Commando Drift Nature Reserve, Tarkastad, 1922 Bulhoek Rebellion, M.C.A. Shepstone 1861, Tylden, Whittlesea, Waqu, Catholic Cross, Sada, Cathcart, Sole, Eastern Cape, Spring Valley, Waterdown Dam, Devil's Bellows, Nico Malan Pass, 1820 Settlers Milestone, Thomas River, Cameron's Glen, Glenrock, Katberg Pass, Balfour, Fort Armstrong, Oakdene, Stutterheim, Dohne, Liddleton, Mpofu N.R., Seymour, Hogsback, Gaika's Grave 1829, Keiskammahoek, Kubusi, Amabele, Bedford, Adelaide, Blinkwater, Fort Hare, Keiskammahoek, Kei Road, Braunschweig, Bofolo, Alice, Middledrift, Rooikrans Dam, BHISHO, Fort Beaufort, Martello Tower, Fort Willshire, Pewuleni, King William's Town, Zwelitsha, Breidbach, Sam Knott Nat. Res., Milkwood Tree, Sittingbourne, Carlisle Bridge, Fort Brown, Great Fish River Conservation Area, Breakfast Vlei, Chalumna, Riebeeck-East, Brakkloof, Andries Vosloo Kudu N.R., Ecca Pass, Committees, Peddie, Bell, GRAHAMSTOWN, Fort Selwyn, Makanas Kop, Wooldridge, Wesley, Hamburg, Alicedale, Shamwari Game Reserve, Thomas Baines Nature Reserve, 1820 Settlers Monument, Salem, Langholm, Fallodon, Bathurst, Nolukhanyo, Ncanara, Kenton-on-Sea, Port Alfred

Copyright © Map Studio 2015

Grid references: CV, CW, CX, CY, CZ

Elevations noted: 2074m, 2106m, 2369m

Route markers: R391, R396, R56, R397, R344, R392, R401, R61, R351, R345, R63, R350, R352, R346, R67, R400, R342, R72, N6, N2

Coordinates: 26°00'E, 27°00'E

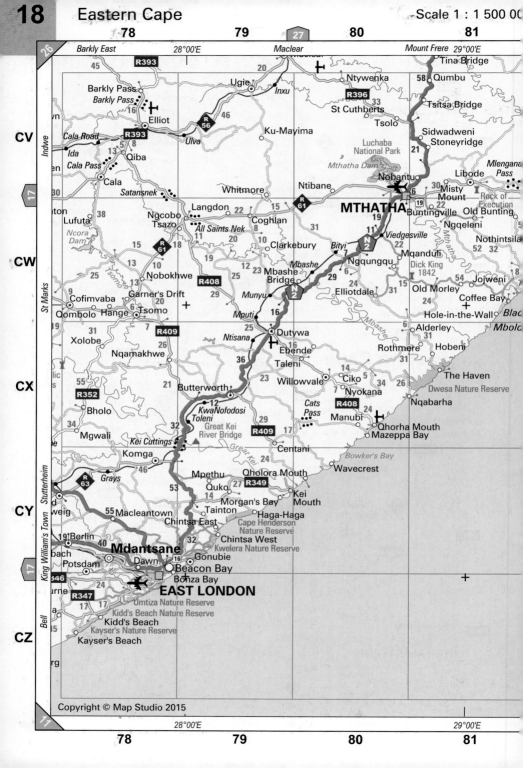

26 Barkly East   28°00'E   Maclear   Mount Frere   29°00'E

R393
45   20   Ntywenka   58   Qumbu   Tina Bridge
Barkly Pass   Ugie   R396   33   Tsitsa Bridge
Barkly Pass   Inxu   St Cuthberts
16   46   Ku-Mayima   Tsolo   Sidwadweni
CV   Elliot   R56   Stoneyridge
R393   Ulva   Luchaba   21
Cala Road   National Park   Mlengana
Ida   13   5   8   Mthatha Dam   Libode   Pass
Cala Pass   Qiba   Nobantu   30   Misty
30   Cala   Ntibane   6   Mount   Rock of
17   Satansnek   Whitmore   MTHATHA   22   Old Bunting   Execution
Langdon   22   15   19   Buntingville   Ngqeleni
Lufuta   38   Ngcobo   R61   11   Nothintsila
CW   Tsazo   Coghlan   31   Viedgesville   52   32
Ncora   All Saints Nek   8   Bityi   22   Mqanduli   Jojweni
Dam   15   R61   18   20   10   Clarkebury   Ngqungqu   Dick King   54
13   10   19   12   23   Mbashe   6   1842   Old Morley   Coffee Bay
25   13   Nobokhwe   R408   25   Mbashe   29   Elliotdale   15   Old Morley
Cofimvaba   Garner's Drift   29   Bridge   24   Hole-in-the-Wall
9   Hange   20   Munyu   16   6   Alderley   Mbolo
Qombolo   6   Tsomo   Mputi   25   Dutywa   31   Hobeni
19   31   Ntisana   16   Rothmere   31   The Haven
Xolobe   26   Ebende   14   Ciko   5   34   Dwesa Nature Reserve
Nqamakhwe   36   Taleni   Nyokana   26   Nqabarha
CX   21   Butterworth   23   Willowvale   7   R408   24   Qhorha Mouth
R352   12   Cats   Manubi   Mazeppa Bay
Bholo   KwaNofodosi   Pass
34   Toleni   29   R409   17   Bowker's Bay
Mgwali   32   Great Kei   Centani   Wavecrest
Kei Cuttings   River Bridge   24   Qholora Mouth
Komga   Great Kei
46   Mpethu   Quko   27   R349
R63   Grays   53   14   Kei
CY   55   Macleantown   Morgan's Bay   Mouth
Berlin   Tainton   Haga-Haga
19   40   Chintsa East   Cape Henderson
Dawn   32   Chintsa West   Nature Reserve
Potsdam   Mdantsane   16   Gonubie   Kwelera Nature Reserve
546   24   Beacon Bay
R347   17   EAST LONDON   Bonza Bay
17   Umtiza Nature Reserve
Kidd's Beach Nature Reserve
CZ   Kidd's Beach
Kayser's Nature Reserve
Kayser's Beach

28°00'E   29°00'E
78   79   80   81

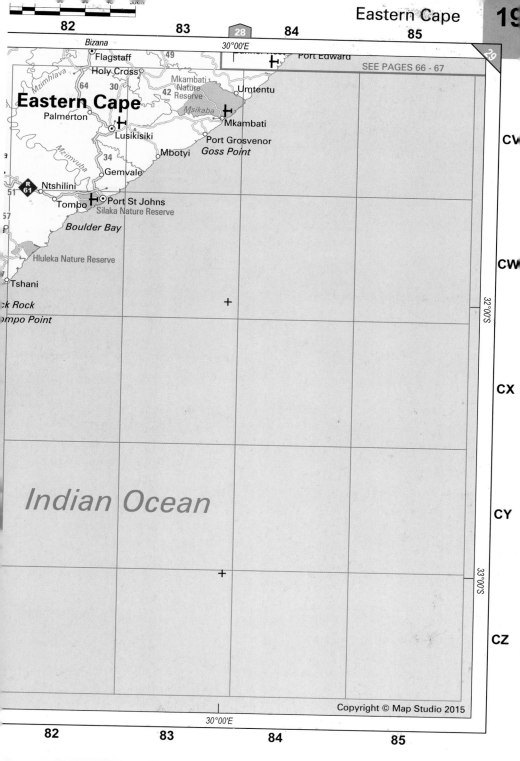

82   83   **28**   84   85

30°00'E

Bizana

Flagstaff

49

Port Edward

Mzimhlava

Holy Cross

Eastern Cape

64   30

Mkambati Nature Reserve

42

Umtentu

29

SEE PAGES 66 - 67

Palmerton

Msikaba

Lusikisiki

Mkambati

34

Port Grosvenor

Mbotyi   *Goss Point*

Gemvale

Mzimvuba

Ntshilini

51

R 61

Tombo

Port St Johns

57

Silaka Nature Reserve

Boulder Bay

Hluleka Nature Reserve

Tshani

ck Rock

ompo Point

+

Indian Ocean

+

CW

CW

32°00'S

CX

CY

33°00'S

CZ

30°00'E

82   83   84   85

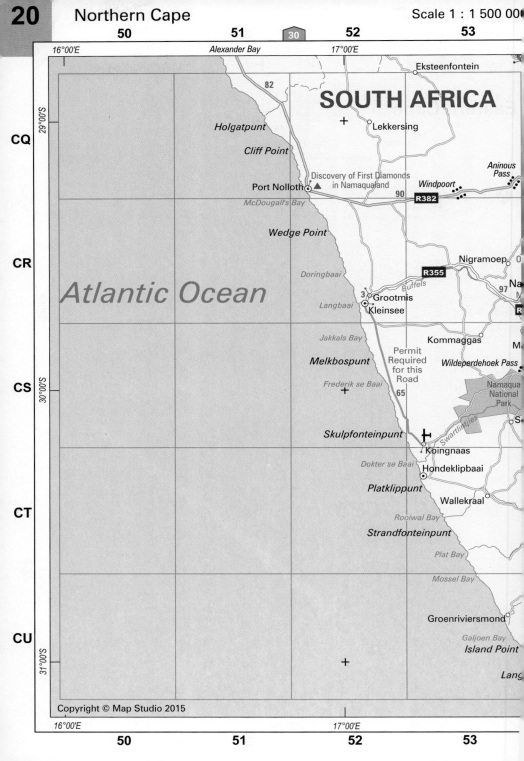

50   51   30   52   53

16°00'E   Alexander Bay   17°00'E

Eksteenfontein

SOUTH AFRICA

82

CQ

Holgatpunt

Lekkersing

Cliff Point

Aninous Pass

Discovery of First Diamonds in Namaqualand

Windpoort

Port Nolloth

90   R382

McDougall's Bay

Wedge Point

Nigramoep   0

CR

Doringbaai

R355

Buffels

97   Na

Langbaai

3   Grootmis
Kleinsee

Atlantic Ocean

Jakkals Bay

Kommaggas

M

Permit Required for this Road

Wildeperdehoek Pass

CS

Melkbospunt

Frederik se Baai

65

Namaqua National Park

S

Skulpfonteinpunt

Swartlintjies

Koingnaas

Dokter se Baai

Hondeklipbaai

CT

Platklippunt

Wallekraal

Rooiwal Bay

Strandfonteinpunt

Plat Bay

Mossel Bay

Groenriviersmond

CU

Galjoen Bay

Island Point

Lang

16°00'E   17°00'E

29°00'S

30°00'S

31°00'S

50   51   52   53

5 10   20   30   40   50km

54   55   31   56   57

18°00'E   D292   19°00'E   31

ordoewer
Vioolsdrif

Orange   NAMIBIA

Goodhouse   Gadiep

Orange

65   N7   Pella

Dabenoris   29°00'S   Pofadder   CQ

Steinkopf   Aggeneys 7   53

Brak   9 7   22

N o r t h e r n   N14   Bloemhoek   Namies

42   **C a p e**   103   CR

Bulletrap   62

picular Diorite Koppie   Concordia   N14   48

10   Goegab   Uitkyk   Pofadder

abeep   Okiep   Nature Reserve

ner's Memorial   7 55   R358   CS

55 **Springbok**

R355   59   Brak   R358

tjieskloof   Mesklip   Rietfontein   30°00'S

Burke's   Buffels   Gamoep

Pass

Messelpad   68   R355

Pass

ebatsfontein   Pypmaker   50

Skilpad Wildflower Gardens   se Poort   50

Kamieskroon   CT

Spoeg   Barter's   Stofvlei

46   Grave 1902   Leliefontein   Platbakkies

Spoegrivier   Methodist   38   35   22

Church 1855   Aalwynsfontein

Karkams   34   Witwater

Groen   N7   10   22

Bitter   Langkloof

Garies   5   K

Grootberg   R355

Nariep   61   1022m   75   CU

Groen   Swart Doring   Ottaspoort   Loeriesfontein

Rooiwalspoort

R358   778m

Kotzesrus   Rietpoort

Western   R357

lip   Bitterfontein   Bitterfontein   **Cape**

Komkans   Paddagat   17

Hoek Bay   Nuwerus   Copyright © Map Studio 2015

18°00'E   Vanrhynsdorp   19°00'E   Brandkop

54   55   12   56   57

Northern Cape

Onseepkans · Nous · Upington · Alheit · Kakamas · Neiler

N14

13 · Bladgrond

Kaboep · 49 · 45

CQ · Springbok 29°00'S · 54 · Pofadder · R358 · 25 · Houmoed

Sout · Hartbees · 84 · Tuins

es · 31

Orange River Wineries

CR · 48 · N7 · Geelvloer · Karvloer · Jagkolkvloer · Doringknie se Vloer · Kolke

Bosduiflaagte · R 27

Dagab

CS · 30°00'S · Granaatboskolk · Karreeboschkolk · Halfweg · Verdorskolk · 142 · Grootvloer

Katkop · Onderstedorings

Konnes se Pan · Dwaggasoutpan · Rietfontein · Rietfontein se Pan · R357 · 61

Commissioner's Salt Pan · Brandvlei

CT · Kromkop · 121 · Rock Paintings · R353 · 47 · Riet se Vloer

Krom · R 27 · Blomberg se Vloer

R357 · Swartkolkvloer · Sakrivier

CU · Windmill Museum · 8 · Tontelbos · R353

10 · Loeriesfontein · 44 · Bodam · 77

R357 · Oumuur · Sak

Brandkop 31°00'S

20°00'S · Calvinia · Williston

58 · 59 · 60 · 61

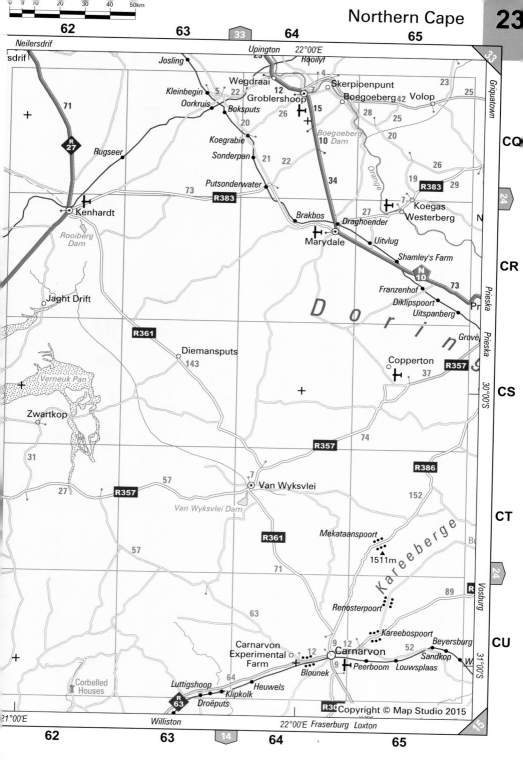

0 5 10 20 30 40 50km

62   63   64   65

33   64   65

Neilersdrif
sdrif
Josling
Upington   22°00'E
Rooilyt
Wegdraai
Kleinbegin   5   22
Oorkruis
Boksputs
Groblershoop
12
Skerpioenpunt
Boegoeberg   42   Volop
23
25
71
20
26   15
28
25
CQ
Rugseer
Koegrabie
Sonderpan   21   22
Boegoeberg   10   Dam
20
24
Putsonderwater
73
R383
34
Boegoeberg
19   R383   29
Kenhardt
26
7
Koegas
Westerberg
Brakbos
27
Draghoender
Marydale   Uitvlug
Shamley's Farm
N   N10
CR
Rooiberg
Dam
73
Franzenhof
Diklipspoort
Uitspanberg
Prieska
Jaght Drift
R361
Dorin
Grovè
Prieska
Diemansputs
143
Copperton
37   R357
30°00'S
Verneuk Pan
CS
Zwartkop
74
R357
31
R386
R357
57
7
Van Wyksvlei
152
27
R357
24
Van Wyksvlei Dam
CT
Mekataanspoort
R361
1511m
57
71
Kareeberge
Vosburg
89
R
Renosterpoort
63
Kareebospoort
Carnarvon
Experimental
Farm
9   12
12
Carnarvon
52
Beyersburg
Sandkop
CU
Blounek
9   Peerboom   Louwsplaas
W
Corbelled
Houses
Luttigshoop
64
Heuwels
Klipkolk
R63
Droëputs
R30   Copyright © Map Studio 2015

21°00'E
Williston
22°00'E   Fraserburg   Loxton

62   63   64   65

Griquatown
33
24
24
15

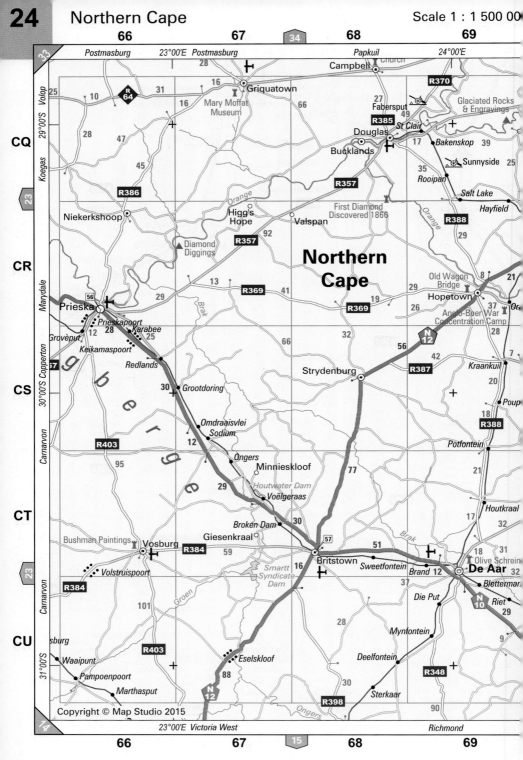

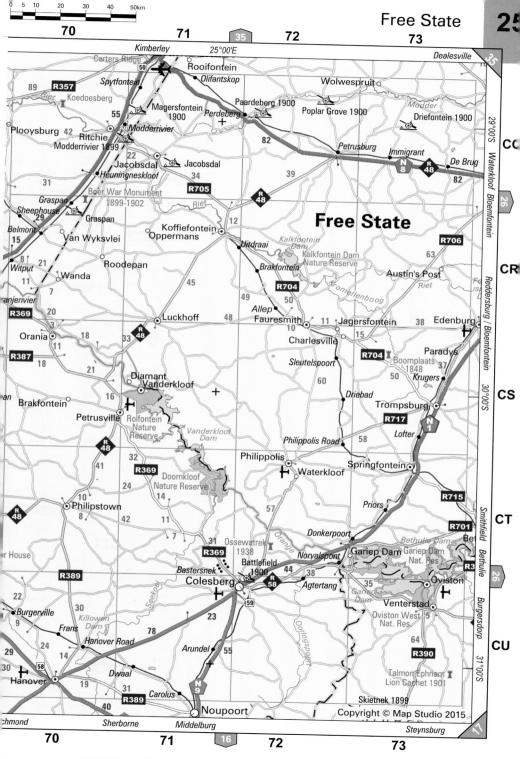

0 5 10 20 30 40 50km

Kimberley

25°00'E

Dealesville

Carters Ridge

Rooifontein

Olifantskop

Wolwespruit

89   R357

Spytfontein

Koedoesberg

Magersfontein 1900

Paardeberg 1900

Perdeberg

Poplar Grove 1900

Modder

Driefontein 1900

29°00'S

Waterkloof / Bloemfontein

CO

55

Plooysburg 42

Ritchie

Modderrivier

Modderrivier 1899

Jacobsdal

Heuningneskloof

22

Jacobsdal

34

39

Petrusburg

Immigrant

N8

De Brug

82

R48

82

31

R705

Boer War Monument 1899-1902

Graspan

Sheephouse

29

Graspan

Riet

R48

Free State

R706

26

CR

Belmont

15

Van Wyksvlei

Koffiefontein

Oppermans

12

Uitdraai

Kalkfontein Dam

Kalkfontein Dam Nature Reserve

63

Austin's Post

Reddersburg / Bloemfontein

Riet

8

21

Witput

11

7

Roodepan

45

Brakfontein

Kromellenboog

R704

Wanda

49

50

Allep

Fauresmith

11

Jagersfontein

38

Edenburg

Oranjerivier

R369

20

3

Luckhoff

48

10

15

Charlesville

Paradys

Orania

18

33

R48

R704

Boomplaats 1848

37

R387

11

18

21

Diamant

Vanderkloof

16

Sleutelspoort

60

Driebad

Krugers

50

30°00'S

CS

Brakfontein

Petrusville

Rolfontein Nature Reserve

Vanderkloof Dam

Trompsburg

R717

N1

Lofter

R48

32

R369

41

Doornkloof Nature Reserve

24

Philippolis Road

58

Springfontein

Philippolis

Waterkloof

Smithfield

R715

CT

10

Philipstown

14

8

42

11

57

Priors

R701

Be

26

7

31

R369

Ossewatrek 1938

Donkerpoort

Orange

Bethulie Dam

Gariep Dam

Gariep Dam Nat. Res

Bethulie

R3

R389

Bastersnek

Battlefield 1900

44

Norvalspont

35

Oviston

Colesberg

R58

38

Agtertang

Gariep Dam

Venterstad

Burgersdorp

22

59

23

Oviston West Nat. Res

5

CU

Burgerville

9

30

Frans

Killowen Dam

64

R390

29

24

78

Hanover Road

14

Arundel

55

Talmon Ephriam Lion Cachet 1901

30

58

Dwaal

19

31

Carolus

Skietnek 1899

Hanover

40

R389

N9

Noupoort

Copyright © Map Studio 2015

chmond

Sherborne

Middelburg

Steynsburg

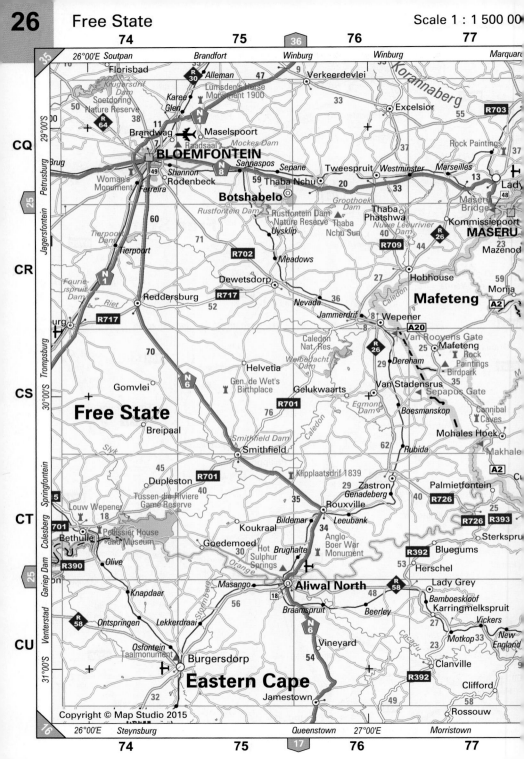

5 10 20 30 40 50km

Panorama   Fouriesburg   Butha-Buthe   Joel's Drift   29°00'E

World Heritage Site)
Rock
Paintings

Qhobela
Prehistoric Footprints
Moteng Pass

Gumtree   Ficksburg
41
R 26
A1
29
Hlotse
(Leribe)
Khabo

Butha-buthe

Maputsoe
6
Fort
13
Corn Exchange
29

Matlameng
Liqhobong

Mothae
Cathedral
Peak

Peka Bridge
Peka

Pitseng

Leribe
A25
34

Kao

Mokhotlong

CQ

Kolonyama
40

Koenong

Lesotho

29°00'S

Mamates

Mapoteng
Nokong

Lejone

Highlands
Water Scheme

Mapholaneng

58
Mokhotlong

28

Teyateyaneng
45

Moletsane

Katse
Reservoir

Berea
57

A14
Thobana
Ntlenyana

Moshoeshoe's
Mountain Fortress

Molimo
Nthuse
Pass

Mohale
Dam

3482m

CR

Thaba Bosiu
12
A3
61

Thaba-Tseka

Roma

Likalaneng

A3
3

A5

Blue
Mountain
Pass

Mohale
Dam

A3

Cheche
Pass

Mokhoabong
Pass

Thaba-Tseka

A4

A3

Matsieng
39

LESOTHO

Police Post

Sehonghong

Bushman's Nek /
Nkonkoana

30°00'S

Maseru

Thaba Putsoa
3095m

72

A5

Semonkong

Sehlabathebe

Sehlabathebe National Park

CS

Nohana

Mokopung

Patlong

Qacha's Nek

Ramatseliso's
Gate

Ketane
42

Tsoelike

Qacha's Nek

obong

31

A4

Mphaki

Qacha's Nek
12
Mafube

**Mohale's
Hoek**

A4

20
Lehlohonolo

Phamong

Sebapala
78

Roamer's
Rest
Sigoga
26

Matatiele
Wembley

New
Amalfi

ing Camp

Tosing

Quthing

Ongeluksnek

Edendale
23

Cedarville
R 56
45

Moyeni (Quthing)

Thaba
Chitja

CT

Telle Bridge
Ralebona

15
Kinirapoort

28

R393

Rock
Paintings

**SOUTH
AFRICA**

Bonn
Ridg

Rock
aintings
61
Lundin's Nek

Colonanek

Mount Fletcher
R405

Naudesnek
58
R396

Lower
Pitseng

Lahlangubo
Moordenaarsnek

Rode
32

CU

Rhodes

Elands Height

Mount Frere
N 2

Naudé's Nek
Monument

Mosheshs Ford
32

Halcyon Drift

**Eastern
Cape**

Barkly East

47

R58
45

R393
49

R396

Maclear

Tina Bridge

20

Ugie

Ntywenka

Barkly Pass

Elliot   28°00'E   Elliot   Tsolo   Tsitsa Bridge   29°00'E

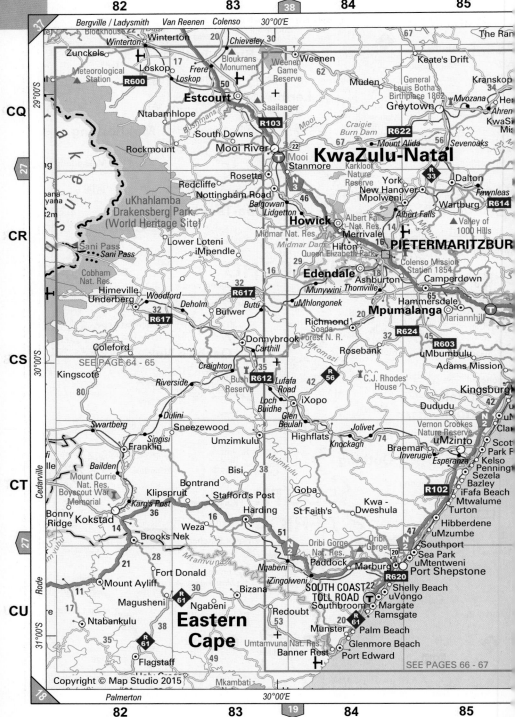

5 10 20 30 40 50km

86   87   **39**   88   89

31°00'E   Nkwalini   Kwa Mbonambi

Indian Ocean

eMpangeni
Richards Bay
Mhlatuzi Lagoon
Richards Bay Nature Reserve
Felixton 29

Bulawayo site of
Shaka's Kraal

h Grave
eNtumeni
eShowe
Fort Nongqai
Fort KwaMondi

Coward's Bush
Monument

uMlalazi Nature Reserve
Mtunzini
Mtunzini

22

Ntunjambili
R102 17

21

hannsburg
Gingindlovu
aMatikulu
Gingindlovu
Dokodweni

Fort Mtombeni
Mapumulo
Timati
Tugela
Mpumulwane
Nyoni
Nyathini 22 T NORTH COAST TOLL ROUTE
Tugela 1838
Mandini
Tugela Mouth

R 74
abantu
ion

40
46 12

Fort Trealork

CQ

ze 1906
Darnall
Ultimatum Tree
Fort Pearson

Mvoti
Shaka's Memorial
Aldinville
Shakaskraal
uMhlali
Zinkwazi Beach

KwaDukuza (Stanger)

17
15
80

Sheffield Beach
Salt Rock
Shaka's Rock
Ballito

CR

Tongaat
iNanda
Ndwedwe
Verulam
NORTH COAST TOLL ROUTE

Kwa-
Mashu
Phoenix
uMdloti
uMhlanga

Clermont
Pinetown
DURBAN
The Bluff
Queensburgh
21

uMlazi
aManzimtoti

gababa
omaas
thal
urgh
nie

CS

CT

CU

29°00'S

30°00'S

31°00'S

SEE PAGES 66 - 67

31°00'E   32°00'E

86   87   88   89

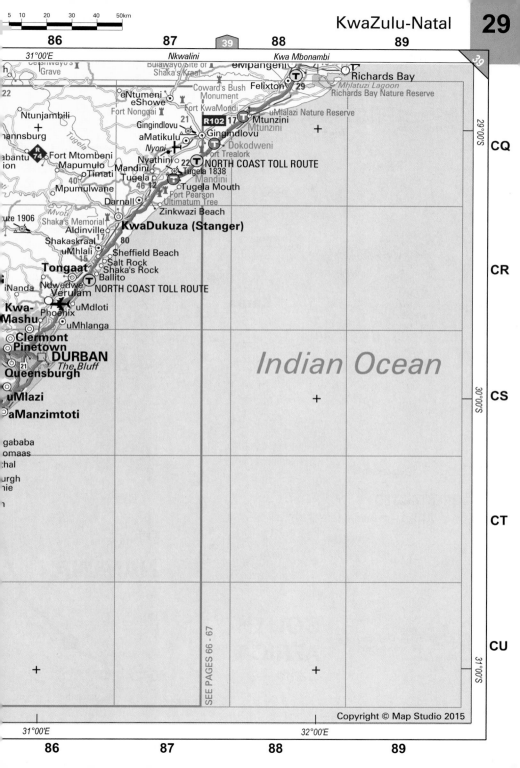

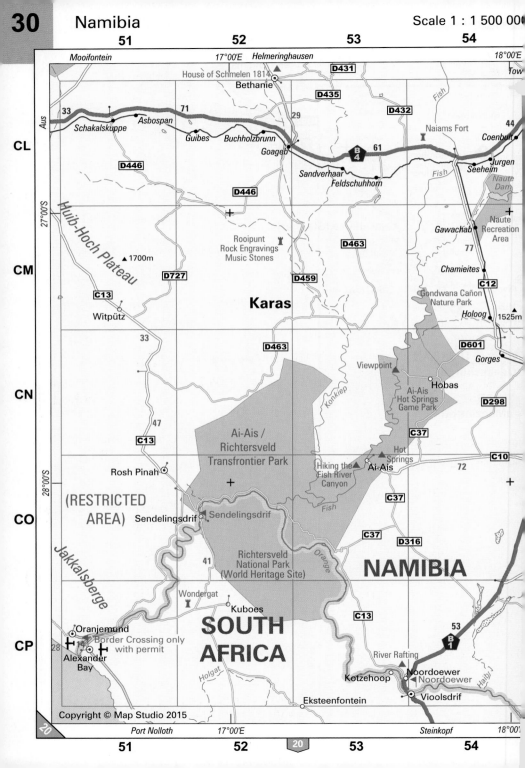

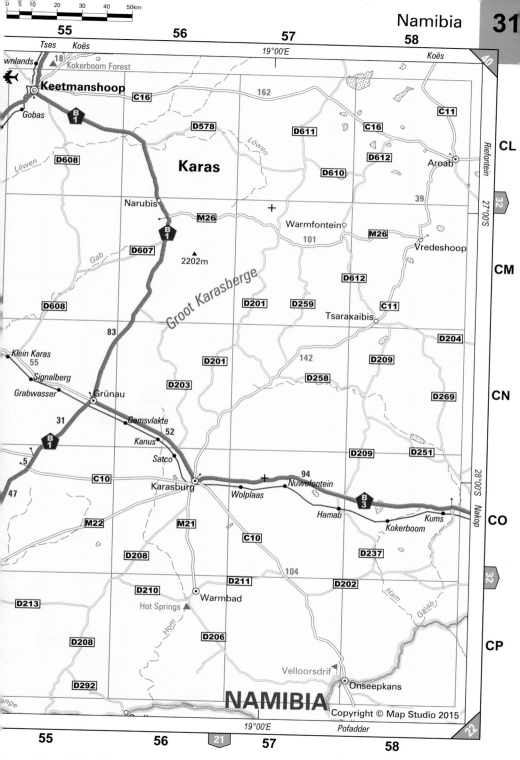

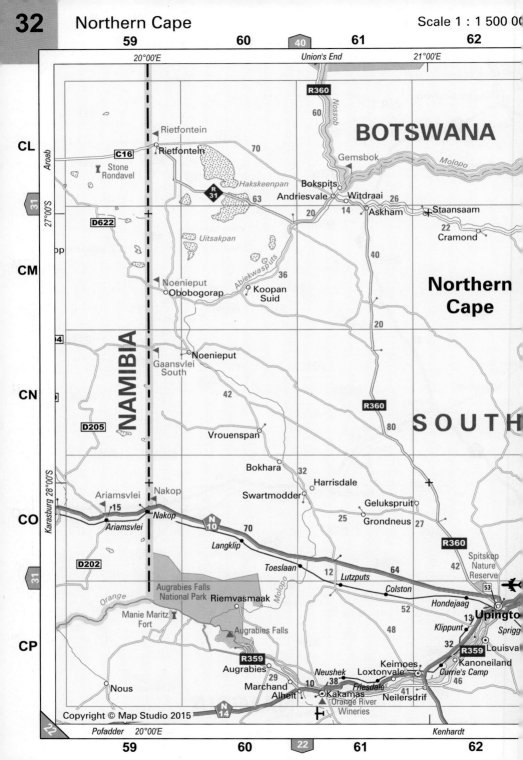

59   60   **40**   61   62

Union's End

20°00'E   21°00'E

R360

60

Nossob

BOTSWANA

CL

Aroab

Rietfontein

C16   Rietfontein

Stone Rondavel

70

Gemsbok   Molopo

Hakskeenpan

R 31   63   Bokspits

31   Andriesvale   Witdraai   26

20   14   Askham   Staansaam

D622   27°00'S

22   Cramond

Uitsakpan

40

CM

Abiekwasputs

36   Koopan Suid

Northern Cape

Noenieput   Obobogorap

20

CN

Noenieput

Gaansvlei South   42

D205

R360   **S O U T H**

80

Vrouenspan

Bokhara   32

Harrisdale

Swartmodder

CO

Karasburg 28°00'S

Ariamsvlei   Nakop

15   Gelukspruit

Ariamsvlei   Nakop   **N 10**   70   25   Grondneus   27

Langklip   **R360**

D202   Toeslaan   12   Lutzputs   64   42   Spitskop Nature Reserve

Orange   Molopo   Colston   **53**

31   Augrabies Falls National Park   Riemvasmaak   52   Hondejaag   Upingto

48   Klippunt   13   Sprigg

Manie Maritz Fort   Augrabies Falls   32   Louisva

CP

R359   Keimoes   Kanoneiland   **R359**

Nous   Augrabies   Neushek   Loxtonvale   Currie's Camp   46

Marchand   10   38   Friesdale   41

Alheit   Kakamas   Neilersdrif

Orange River Wineries

N 14

22

Pofadder   20°00'E   Kenhardt

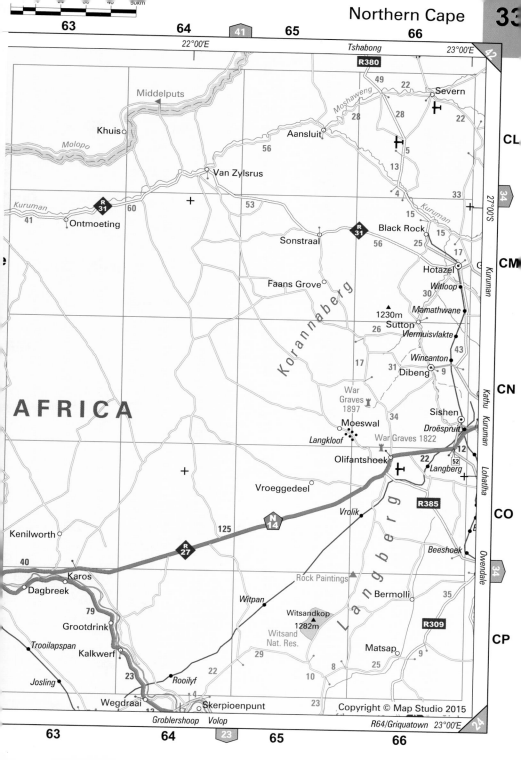

Middelputs

Khuis

Molopo

Van Zylsrus

Kuruman

Ontmoeting

56

Sonstraal

Faans Grove

Aansluit

Tshabong

R380

49

22

Severn

28

28

22

5

13

4

33

15

Black Rock

15

56

25

17

Hotazel

Witloop

30

Mamathwane

1230m

Sutton

26

Vlermuisvlakte

43

Wincanton

31

Dibeng

9

AFRICA

War Graves 1897

Moeswal

Langkloof

War Graves 1822

Olifantshoek

Vroeggedeel

Kenilworth

40

Karos

Dagbreek

79

Grootdrink

Trooilapspan

Kalkwerf

23

Josling

Rooilyf

Wegdraai

Volop

Groblershoop

Sishen

Droëspruit

12

22

52

Langberg

34

17

41

53

60

31

125

N14

R27

Vrolik

R385

Beeshoek

Rock Paintings

Bermolli

35

Witpan

Witsandkop

1282m

Witsand
Nat. Res.

Matsap

R309

9

29

8

25

10

22

4

Skerpioenpunt

23

Copyright © Map Studio 2015

R64/Griquatown

Korannaberg

Langberg

Kuruman

Kathu

Lohatha

Owendale

CL

CM

CN

CO

CP

22°00'E

23°00'E

27°00'S

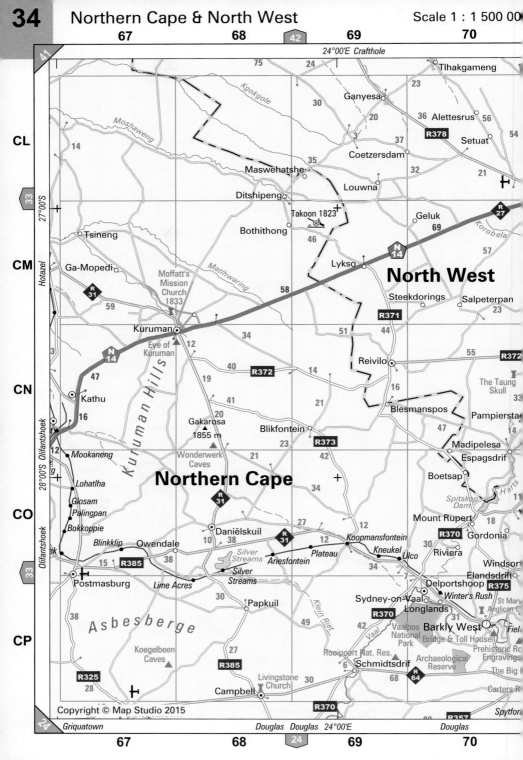

67   68   42   69   70

24°00'E Crafthole

75   24   Tlhakgameng

CL

Kgokgole

Ganyesa   23

Moshaweng

30   20   36 Alettesrus   56

3   37   R378   Setuat   54

14   35   Coetzersdam   32   21

Maswehatshe

Louwna

Ditshipeng   Takoon 1823   R27

CM   Tsineng   Bothithong   46   Geluk   69   Korobela

Hotazel

Ga-Mopedi   Lykso   **North West**

R31   Matlhwaring   58   N14   57

59   Moffatt's Mission Church 1833   Steekdorings   Salpeterpan

Kuruman   R371   23

Eye of Kuruman   12   34   51   44   55   R372

N14   40   R372   Reivilo   The Taung Skull

CN   47   19   14   33

Kathu   41   16   Pampiersta

16   Gakarosa   20   21   Blesmanspos

12   1855 m   Blikfontein   47   14

Mookaneng   Wonderwerk Caves   23   R373   Madipelesa   Espagsdrif

Lohatlha   **Northern Cape**   21   42   Boetsap

CO   Glosam   34   Harts

Palingpan   Spitskop Dam

Bokkoppie   R31   Mount Rupert   18

Blinkklip   27   12   R370   Gordonia

Owendale   Daniëlskuil   Koopmansfontein   30   Riviera

15   R385   10   38   R31   12   Kneukel   Windsor

38   Silver Streams   Ariesfontein   Plateau   Ulco   Elandsdrift

Postmasburg   Lime Acres   Silver Streams   34   7   Delportshoop   R375

Olifantshoek

30   Papkuil   Sydney-on-Vaal   Winter's Rush   St Mary Anglican C

CP   38   49   42   Longlands   31   Fiel

Asbesberge   R370   Barkly West

Koegelbeen Caves   27   Vaalbos National Park   Bridge & Toll House   Prehistoric Ro Engravings

R325   R385   Rooipoort Nat. Res.   Archaeological Reserve   The Big

28   Livingstone Church   6   Schmidtsdrif   Carters R

Campbell   30   68   R64

R370   R357   Spytfor

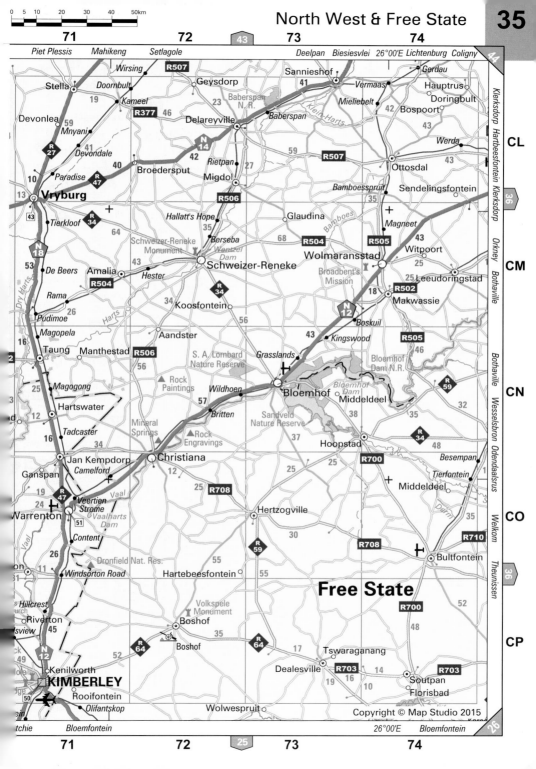

Free State

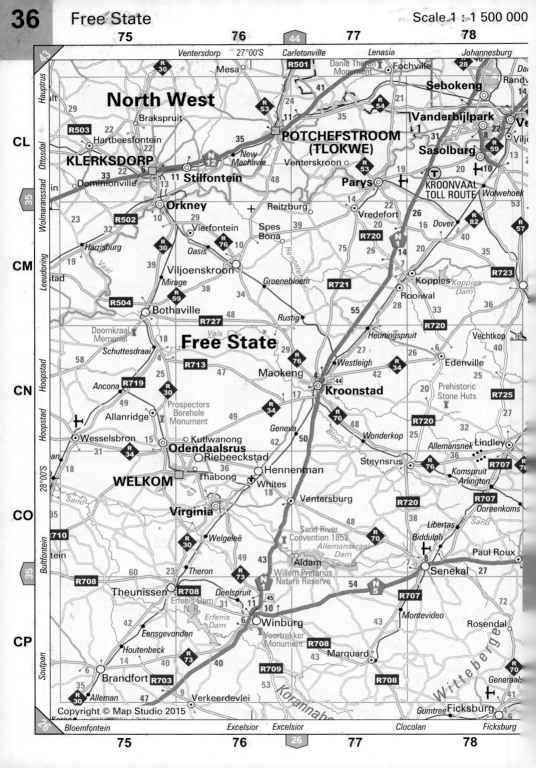

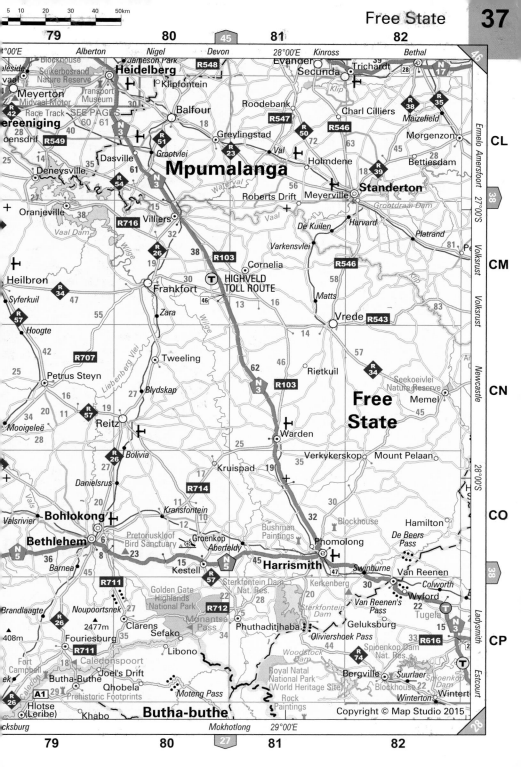

5 10 20 30 40 50km

79 80 45 81 82

°00'E Alberton Nigel Devon 28°00'E Kinross Bethal

R548
Heidelberg
Klipfontein
Blockhouse
Suikerbosrand
Nature Reserve
Jameson Park
Transport
Museum
Midvaal Motor
Meyerton
Race Track
SEE PAGE
60 - 61
ereeniging
R42
40
oensdrif
R549
25 14
Deneysville
54
61
Heilbron
R34
Syferkuil
R57
Hoogte
42
25
R707
Petrus Steyn
16
R57
19
Mooigeleë
Reitz
28
R26
Bolivia
27
Danielsrus
20

Balfour
18
51
23
Grootvlei
Dasville
35
Villiers
R716
32
38
26
19
30
Frankfort
46
Zara
55
Tweeling
27
Blydskap
11
17
Kransfontein
10
12

Mpumalanga

Roodebank
R547
Greylingstad
Val
Holmdene
Waterval
Roberts Drift
De Kuilen
Varkensvlei
R546
Cornelia
58
13
16
Matts
62
46
Rietkuil
35
25
Warden
Verkykerskop
19
Kruispad

R546
50
72
63
45
39
18
Meyerville
Standerton
Harvard
Platrand
81
R543
Vrede
14
57
R34
Seekoeivlei
Nature Reserve
Memel
45
Mount Pelaan

Free
State

Bohlokong
Valsrivier
Bethlehem
N5
36
Barnea
45
R711
Brandlaagte
R26
Noupoortsnek
2477m
408m
Fourieburg
R711
Fort
Campbell
18
Caledonspoort
ek
Butha-Buthe
Qhobela
Prehistoric Footprints
R26
Hlotse
(Leribe)
cksburg Khabo Butha-buthe

6
8
23
Groenkop
Aberfeldy
15
Kestell
R57
Pretoriuskloof
Bird Sanctuary
Golden Gate
Highlands
National Park
R712
Clarens
Sefako
Monantsa
Pass
Libono
Joel's Drift
Moteng Pass

Charl Cilliers
38
35
Maizefield
Morgenzon
28
Bettiesdam

CL

27°00'S

Volksrust

CM

Volksrust

CN

Newcastle

28°00'S

CO

Hamilton
De Beers
Pass
30
Van Reenen
Colworth
Wyford
22
Tugela
15

Blockhouse
Phomolong
R714
32
30
45
Harrismith
47
Swinburne
Sterkfontein Dam
Nat. Res.
22
28
20
Sterkfontein
Dam
Van Reenen's
Pass
Geluksburg
5
Phuthaditjhaba
44
Oliviershoek Pass
Spioenkop Dam
Nat. Res.
R74
Bergville
Suurlaer
Woodstock
Dam
Royal Natal
National Park
(World Heritage Site)
Rock
Paintings
33
R616
Winterton
Wintert

CP

Bushman
Paintings

Spioenkop
Dam

Kerkenberg

Ladysmith

Estcourt

HIGHVELD
TOLL ROUTE

R103

N3

N3

Wilge

R103

Liebenberg Vlei

Vals

Mokhotlong 29°00'E

79 80 27 81 82

Ermelo Amersfoort

46

38

38

28

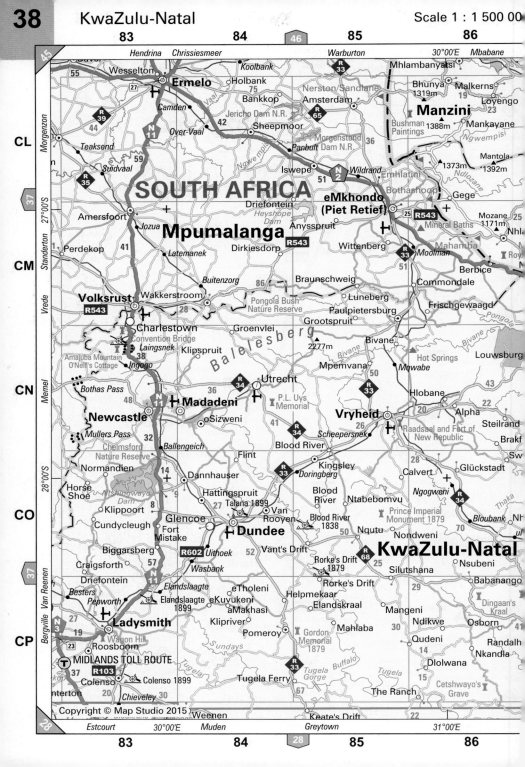

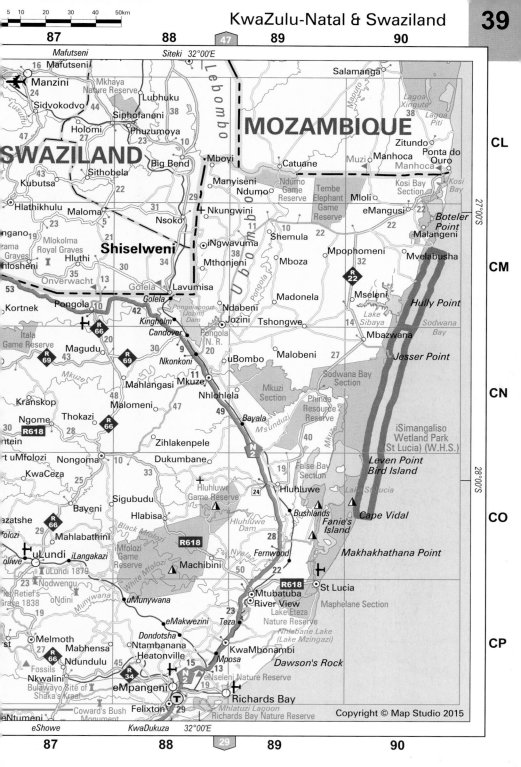

Mafutseni
Siteki 32°00'E

16 Mafutseni
Manzini
24
Mkhaya
Nature Reserve
Lubhuku
Sidvokodvo 44
Siphofaneni
38
Holomi
Phuzumoya
27
10
47
Big Bend
Mboyi
Catuane
Salamanga

Kubutsa
SWAZILAND
43
Sithobela
22
Manyiseni
Ndumo
Hlathikhulu Maloma
31
Nsoko
Nkungwini
11
Shemula 22
23
5
Nsoko
iNgwavuma
ngano 19
21
Mthonjeni
38
Mboza
hloseni
Mlokolma
Royal Graves
Hluthi
30
34
Madonela
Onverwacht 13
Golela Lavumisa
Golela
Pongola 10
42
Kortnek
Kingholm
Candover
Itala
Game Reserve
Magudu
20
30
9
Nkonkoni
20
uBombo
Malobeni 27
Mahlangasi Mkuze
11
Kranskop
48
Malomeni
47
Nhlohlela
Ngome
Thokazi
49
Bayala
ntein
28
Zihlakenpele
t uMfolozi
Nongoma
10
Dukumbane
KwaCeza
25
33
Sigubudu
Bayeni
Hlabisa
Hluhluwe
Game Reserve
Hluhluwe
azatshe
29
Mahlabathini
Black Mfolozi
Hlabisa
Hluhluwe
Dam
oliwe uLundi iLangakazi
iMfolozi
Game
Reserve
R618
Machibini
50
23 Nodwengu
oNdini
White Mfolozi
19
uMunywana
eMakwezini
Teza
Melmoth
Dondotsha
27
Mabhensa
Ntambanana
Nkwalini
Ndundulu
45
Heatonville
Mposa
Bulawayo Site of
Shaka's Kraal
eMpangeni
Felixton
Coward's Bush
Monument
eShowe
KwaDukuza 32°00'E

87 88 89 90

MOZAMBIQUE

Maputo
Lagoa
Xingute
Lagoa
Piti
Zitundo
Manhoca Ponta do
Muzi Manhoca Ouro
Ndumo
Game
Reserve
Tembe
Elephant
Game
Reserve
Mloli
Kosi Bay
Section
Kosi
Bay
eMangusi
22
Boteler
Point
Malangeni
Mpophomeni
32
Mvelabusha
Mseleni
Hully Point
Lake
Sibaya
Mbazwana
Sodwana
Bay
Jesser Point
Sodwana Bay
Section
Phinda
Resource
Reserve
40
iSimangaliso
Wetland Park
(St Lucia) (W.H.S.)
False Bay
Section
Leven Point
Bird Island
Lake St Lucia
Bushlands
Fanie's
Island
Cape Vidal
Fernwood
Makhakhathana Point
St Lucia
Mtubatuba
River View
Lake Eteza
Nature Reserve
Maphelane Section
KwaMbonambi
Dawson's Rock
eNseleni Nature Reserve
Richards Bay
Mhlatuzi Lagoon
Richards Bay Nature Reserve

CL

CM

CN

CO

CP

27°00'S

28°00'S

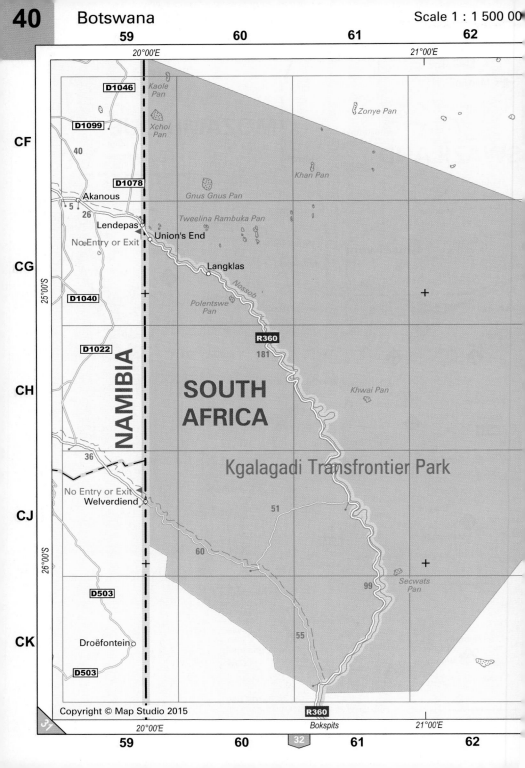

59 60 61 62

20°00'E 21°00'E

D1046
Kaole Pan

Zonye Pan

D1099

CF

Xchoi Pan

40

Khan Pan

D1078

Akanous
Gnus Gnus Pan

5
26

Lendepas
Tweelina Rambuka Pan

Union's End
No Entry or Exit

CG

25°00'S

Langklas

Nossob

D1040
Polentswe Pan

R360
181

NAMIBIA

D1022

SOUTH
AFRICA

CH

Khwai Pan

Kgalagadi Transfrontier Park

36

No Entry or Exit
Welverdiend

CJ

51

26°00'S

60

99
Secwats Pan

D503

55

Droëfontein

CK

D503

20°00'E

R360
Bokspits

21°00'E

59 60 32 61 62

31

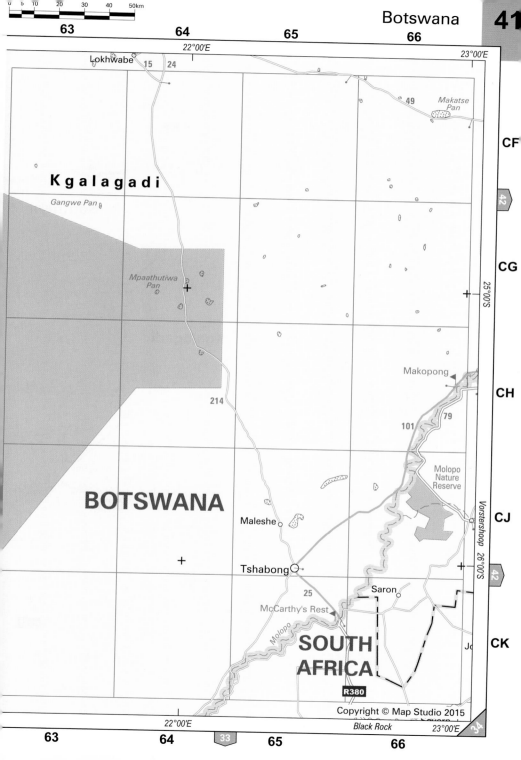

0 5 10 20 30 40 50km

22°00'E 23°00'E

Lokhwabe

15 24

49

Makatse Pan

CF

Kgalagadi

42

Gangwe Pan

CG

Mpaathutiwa Pan

25°00'S

Makopong

CH

214

79

101

Molopo Nature Reserve

BOTSWANA

Vorstershoop

Maleshe

CJ

26°00'S

42

Tshabong

25

Saron

McCarthy's Rest

CK

Molopo

SOUTH AFRICA

Jo

R380

Black Rock

22°00'E 23°00'E

34

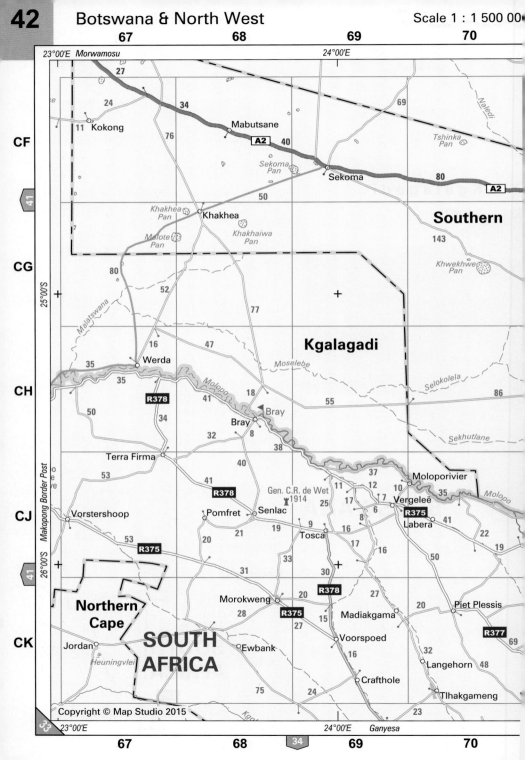

67 **68** **69** **70**

23°00'E Morwamosu 24°00'E

27

24 34
11 Kokong Mabutsane 69
76 A2 40 Tshinka
Pan
CF
Sekoma
Pan Sekoma 80
50 A2
Khakhea
Pan Khakhea **Southern**
143
Malote Khakhaiwa
Pan Pan Khwekhwe
Pan
CG
80
52 + +
25°00'S 77

16 47 **Kgalagadi**
35 Werda Moselebe
35
R378 18 Selokolela 86
41 55
34 Bray
50 Bray Sekhutlane
32 8
CH 38
Terra Firma 40
53 37 Moloporivier Molopo
41 11 12 10 35
R378 Gen. C.R. de Wet 17 7 Vergeleë
Pomfret Senlac 1914 25 6 R375 41
Vorstershoop 19 9 8 Labera 22
53 20 21 Tosca 16 19
R375 17 16
31 50
26°00'S + 33 30 +
Northern R378
Cape 20 27 20 Piet Plessis
Morokweng 15 Madiakgama
28 R375 R377
Jordan **SOUTH** 27 Voorspoed 69
AFRICA 32
Ewbank 16 Langehorn 48
Heuningvlei Crafthole
75 24 Tlhakgameng
23
Copyright © Map Studio 2015
23°00'E 24°00'E Ganyesa

67 **68** **69** **70**

CH
CJ
CK

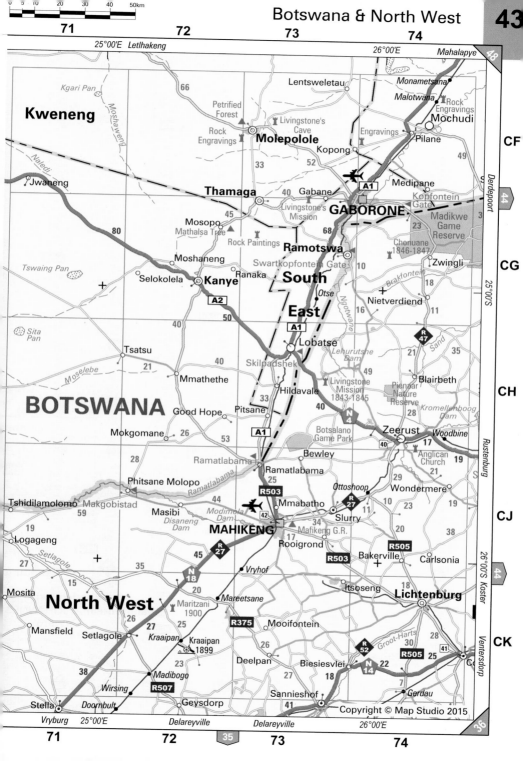

0 5 10   20   30   40   50km

71   72   73   74

25°00'E Letlhakeng   26°00'E   Mahalapye   48

Kweneng

Kgari Pan

66   Lentsweletau   Monametsana
                                             Malotwana   Rock
                                                                Engravings
Petrified   Mochudi
Forest   Livingstone's
Rock   Cave   Engravings   Pilane
Engravings   **Molepolole**   CF
                Kopong
                                             49   Derdepoort
33   52

Jwaneng   A1   Medipane   44
                                             Kopfontein
Thamaga   40   Gabane   **GABORONE**   Gate   3
                45   Livingstone's   Madikwe
Mosopo   Mission   Game
Mathalsa Tree   68   23   Reserve
80   Chenuane
          Rock Paintings   **Ramotswa**   1846-1847   CG
Moshaneng   Swartkopfontein Gate   10   Zwingli
Tswaing Pan   Ranaka   **South**   18
Selokolela   **Kanye**   Nietverdiend   11
                                    Otse   16
Sita   A2   **East**   R47   21   35   CG→CH
Pan   50   A1   Lehurutshe
                                    Dam   21
40   Lobatse
Tsatsu   40   Skilpadshek   Livingstone   49   Blairbeth   CH
21   Mmathethe   33   Hildavale   Mission   Pienaar   28
BOTSWANA   Good Hope   Pitsane   40   1843-1845   Nature   Kromellenboog
                                    A1   Reserve   Dam
Mokgomane   26   53   Botsalano   N4   28
28   Bewley   Game Park   **Zeerust**   Woodbine   CH
Ramatlabama   40   17
Phitsane Molopo   25   **Ramatlabama**   Anglican   19
Tshidilamolomo Makgobistad   44   R503   29   Church   21
59   Masibi   Modimola   Mmabatho   Ottoshoop   Wondermere   CJ
19   Disaneng   Dam   42   R27   10   23   19
Logageng   Dam   34   Slurry   11
27   **MAHIKENG**   Mafikeng G.R.   20   38
45   R27   Rooigrond   17   R505
15   N18   Vryhof   Bakerville   Carlsonia   CJ
North West   20   Mareetsane   Itsoseng   18   R503
Mosita   Maritzani   Mooifontein   **Lichtenburg**   CK
Mansfield   Setlagole   1900   R375   R52   30   28
27   25   Kraaipan   R505   25   41
38   23   Kraaipan   26   N14   22   CK
Madibogo   1899   Deelpan   7
Wirsing   R507   Biesiesvlei   18   Gerdau
Stella   Doornbult   Geysdorp   Sannieshof
Vryburg   25°00'E   Delareyville   41   Delareyville   26°00'E   Copyright © Map Studio 2015   36

71   72   35   73   74

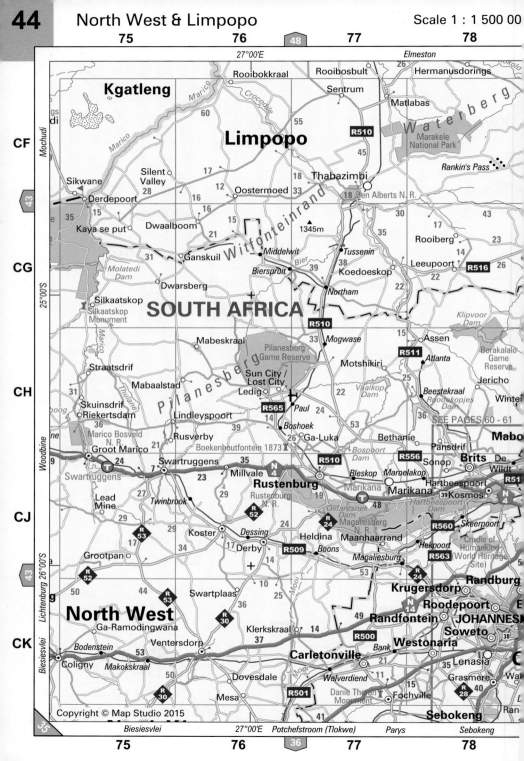

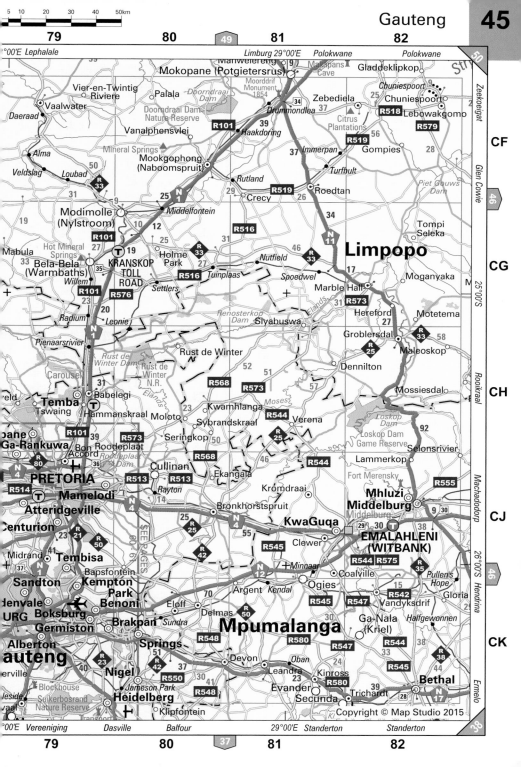

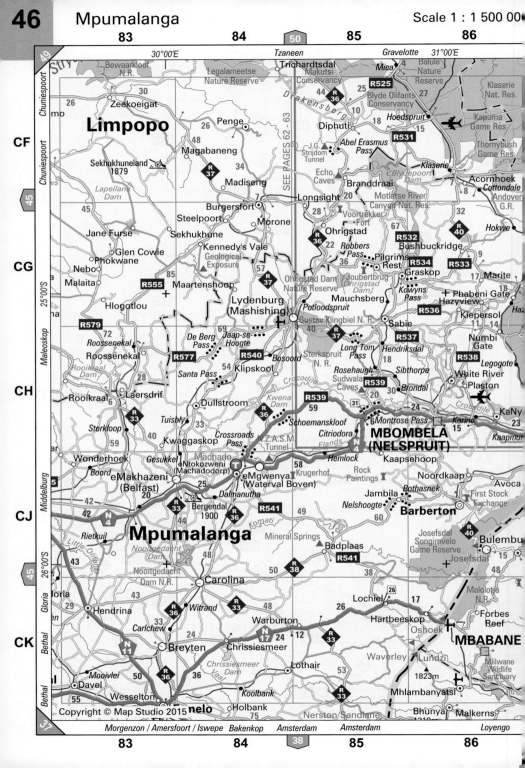

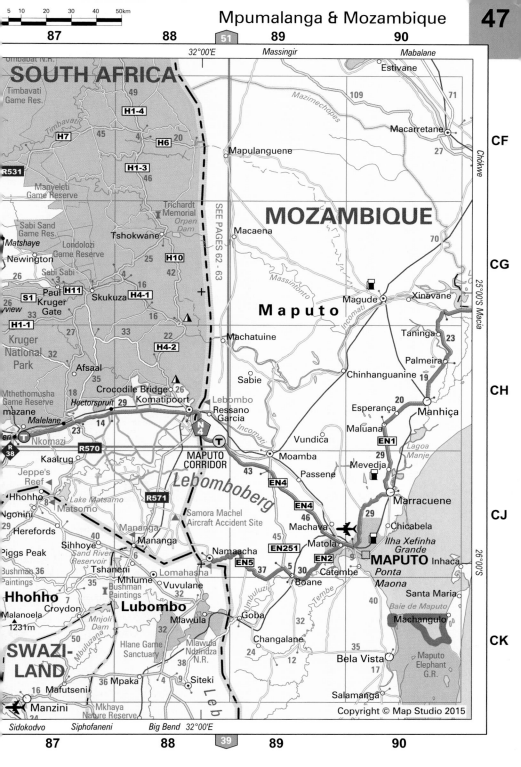

5 10 20 30 40 50km

87 51 88 89 90

32°00'E Massingir Mabalane

SOUTH AFRICA
Umbabat N.R.
Timbavati
Game Res.
49
H1-4
H7 45 4 H6 20
Mapulanguene
H1-3
R531 46
Manyeleti
Game Reserve
Trichardt
Memorial
Tshokwane Orpen
Dam
Matshaye Londolozi
Newington Game Reserve
26 Sabi Sand 25 H10
Game Res. 42
3 16
Sabi Sabi 4
S1 Paul H11 Skukuza H4-1
26 Kruger
view 33 Gate 16
H1-1 27 33 22
Kruger H4-2
National 32
Park Afsaal
35
Mthethomusha 18 Crocodile Bridge 26
Game Reserve Hectorspruit 29 Komatipoort Lebombo
mazane Ressano
Malelane Garcia
en T 23 14 T
Nkomazi MAPUTO
R CORRIDOR
38 Kaalrug R570
Jeppe's Lebomboberg 43
Reef
Hhohho Lake Matsamo R571
Ngonini Matsomo
29 Herefords 40 Mananga
Piggs Peak 6 Mananga
Bushman 36 Sihhoye Sand River
Paintings Reservoir Tshaneni Namaacha
35 Mhlume Lomahasha EN5
Hhohho 7 Bushman Vuvulane
Croydon Paintings 32
Malanoela Lubombo
1231m Mnjoli Mlawula
SWAZI- Dam Goba
50 Hlane Game
LAND Sanctuary Mlawula 32
Ndzindza Changalane
Mkhaya N.R. 24
Nature Reserve 38 Mpaka 4 Siteki
16 Mafutseni
Manzini
24

Estivane
Mazimechopes 109 71
Macarretane
27
Mapulanguene
MOZAMBIQUE
Macaena 70
Massintonto
M a p u t o Magude Xinavane
Incomati Taninga 23
Palmeira
Machatuine Chinhanguanine 19
20
Sabie Esperança Manhiça
Maluana EN1
Vundica Lagoa
Moamba 29 Manje
Passene Mevedja
EN4 45 29 Marracuene
EN4 46 Chicabela
Machava Ilha Xefinha
EN251 Matola Grande
EN2 9 **MAPUTO** Inhaca
37 5 30 Catembe Ponta
Boane Maona
Tembe 40 Santa Maria
Baie de Maputo
Machangulo
35
Bela Vista Maputo
17 Elephant
G.R.
Salamanga

Copyright © Map Studio 2015

CF
CG
CH
CJ
CK

25°00'S Macia Chokwe

26°00'S

Sidokodvo Siphofaneni Big Bend 32°00'E

87 39 88 89 90

SEE PAGES 62 - 63

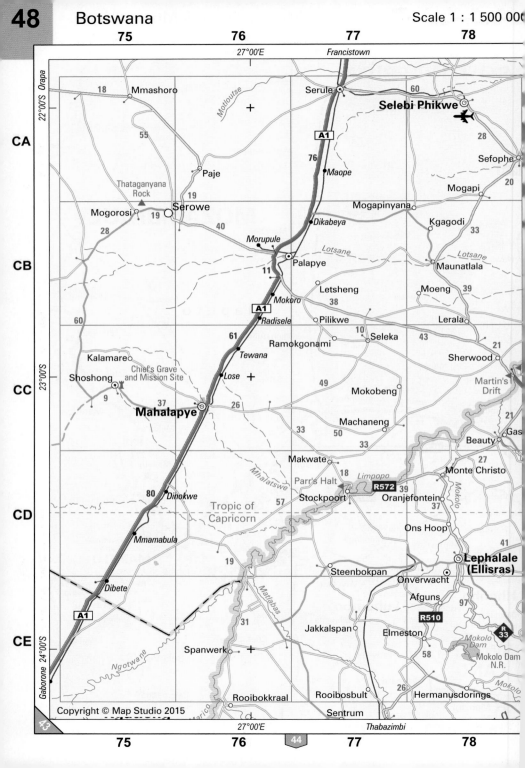

75   76   77   78

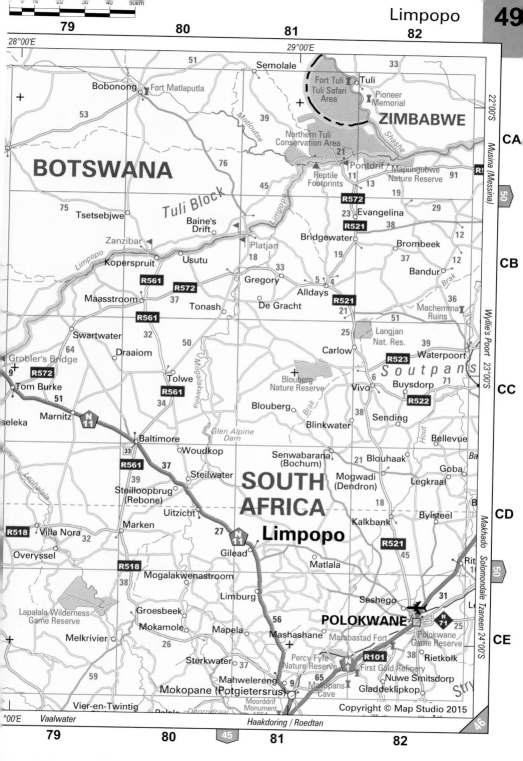

5okm

79   80   81   82

28°00'E   29°00'E

51   Semolale   33
Bobonong   Fort Matlaputla   Fort Tuli   Tuli
                                        Tuli Safari   Pioneer
                                        Area   Memorial

53   39   Northern Tuli   ZIMBABWE
                                        Conservation Area

BOTSWANA   76   21
                                        Pontdrif   Mapungubwe
                                45   Reptile   11   Nature Reserve   91   R
                                        Footprints   13   19
75   Tsetsebjwe   Tuli Block   R572
                                                23   Evangelina   29
        Baine's   R521   38   12
        Drift   Bridgewater   Brombeek
Zanzibar   Platjan   37   12
        Koperspruit   Usutu   18   19   Bandur
R561   33   Brak
        R572   Gregory   5   4
Maasstroom   37   Tonash   De Gracht   Alldays   R521   36
R561   21   Machemma
                                                51   Ruins
Swartwater   32   50   25
Draaiom   Carlow   Langjan   39   Waterpoort
64   Nat. Res.
Grobler's Bridge   Blouberg   R523   71
9   Tolwe   Nature Reserve   Vivo   Buysdorp   Soutpans
R572   R561   Blouberg   6
Tom Burke   34   R522
51   38   Sending
Marnitz   Blinkwater
seleka   N11 Baltimore   Glen Alpine   Bellevue   Ba
        33   Dam   Senwabarana   Hout
        R561   37   Woudkop   (Bochum)   21   Blouhaak
        39   Steilwater   Goba
Steiloopbrug   Mogwadi   Legkraal
(Rebone)   (Dendron)
        Uitzicht   **SOUTH**   18   Bylsteel   B
R518   **AFRICA**   Kalkbank
Villa Nora   32   Marken   27   N   **Limpopo**   R521
Overyssel   Gilead   45
R518   Matlala   Rit
        38   Mogalakwenastroom   Lo
                                        Seshego   31
Lapalala Wilderness   Limburg   25
Game Reserve   Groesbeek   56   **POLOKWANE**   Polokwane
Mokamole   Mapela   Mashashana   Marabastad Fort   Game Reserve
Melkrivier   26   Percy Fyfe   R101   38   Rietkolk
                Nature Reserve   N1   Nuwe Smitsdorp
59   Sterkwater   37   First Gold Refinery   Gladdeklipkop
                Mahwelereng   65   Makapans   Stry
Vier-en-Twintig   Mokopane (Potgietersrus)   9   Cave
                        Moorddrif   Copyright © Map Studio 2015
Vaalwater   Monument   Haakdoring / Roedtan

79   80   81   82

CA
CB
CC
CD
CE

Musina (Messina)   Wyllie's Poort   Makhado   Solomondale Tzaneen
22°00'S   23°00'S   24°00'S

Limpopo
Motloutse
Shashe
Brak
Mogalakwena
Lephalala

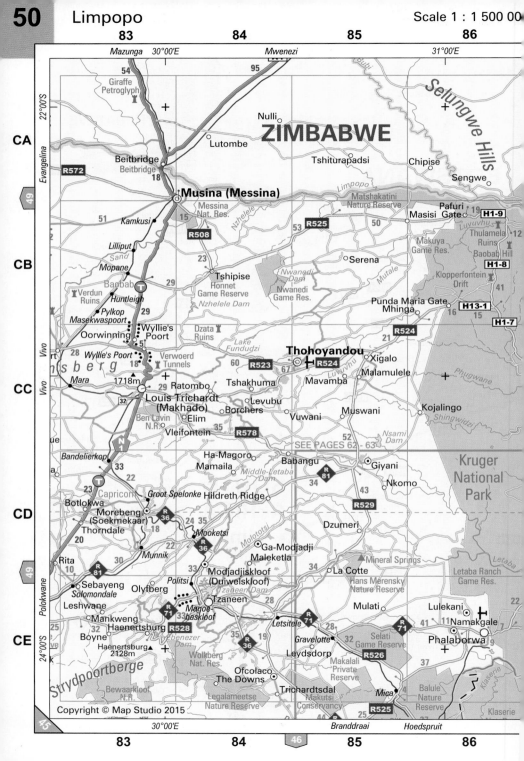

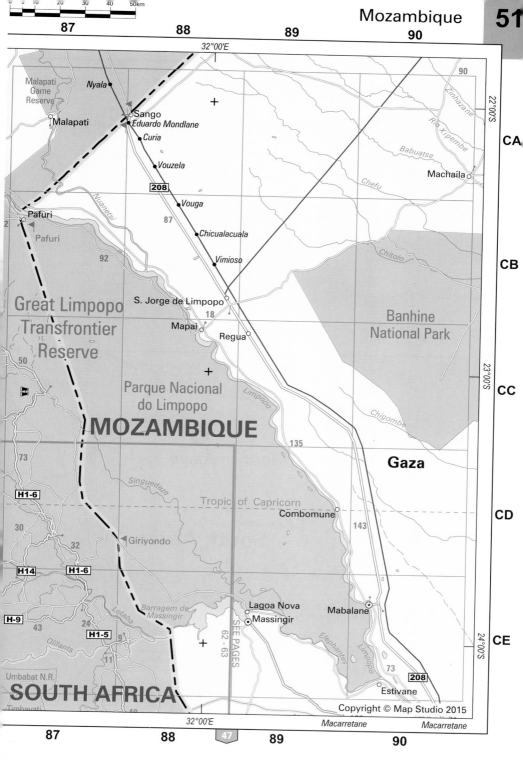

0 5 10 20 30 40 50km

87   88   89   90

32°00'E

90

22°00'S   **CA**

Malapati
Game
Reserve

Nyala

Sango

○Malapati   Eduardo Mondlane

Curia

Zinhlazane

Rio Xipembe

Babuatse

Vouzela

Chefu

Machaila

208

Vouga

Nuanetsi

87

Chicualacuala

○Pafuri

2

Pafuri

92

Vimioso

Chitolo

CB

S. Jorge de Limpopo

Banhine
National Park

**Great Limpopo
Transfrontier
Reserve**

18

Mapai

Regua

50

23°00'S   **CC**

Parque Nacional
do Limpopo

MOZAMBIQUE

Limpopo

Chigombe

73

Singuedeze

135

Gaza

H1-6

Tropic of Capricorn

Combomune

30

143

32

◄Giriyondo

CD

H14   **H1-6**

H-9

43

24

Barragem de
Massingir

Letaba

9

Lagoa Nova

Massingir

Mabalane

H1-5

11

Olifants

SEE PAGES
62 - 63

73

208

Umbabat N.R.

SOUTH AFRICA

Estivane

Elephantes

Limpopo

24°00'S   **CE**

Timbavati

32°00'E

47

Macarretane   Macarretane

87   88   89   90

Legend to Tourist Area Maps

Tarred Untarred Under Construction	Freeway / National Road	▢	Capital or City
	Main Road	◎	Major Town
	Secondary Road	○	Secondary Town
N1 21 R110	Route Numbers	⊙	Other Town
T T	Toll Route and Toll Plaza	○	Settlement
	Mountain Pass	⚔	Battlefields
15	Distance in Kilometres	🏠	Accommodation
	Railway with Station	⌶	Historical Site
	International Boundary	◀	Border Control
	Provincial Boundary	▲	Major Spot Height
	Water Feature	▲	Place of Interest
	Pan	═	Waterfall
	Marsh	⌇	Lighthouse
	National Park / Nature Reserve	🍇	Wine Estate
✈	Major Airport	⍭	Wine Sales
✠	Airfield		

Namibia
B1
Upington
N10
N14
KIMBERLEY

Springbok
N14
R27
Northern Cape
N10
De Aa

South Africa
N12
N1

ATLANTIC
OCEAN
N7
Graaff-Reinet
Beaufort
West
N9

56 - 57
Malmesbury
N1
Western Cape
N12

54 - 55
CAPE TOWN
N2
Riversdale
Knysna
N2
58 - 59
Bredasdorp

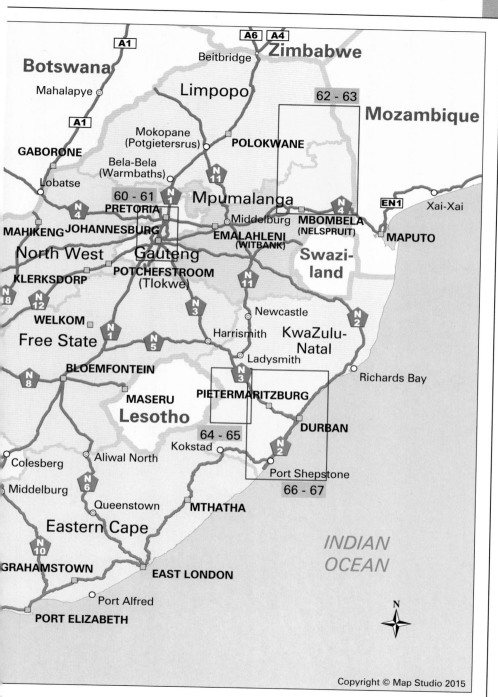

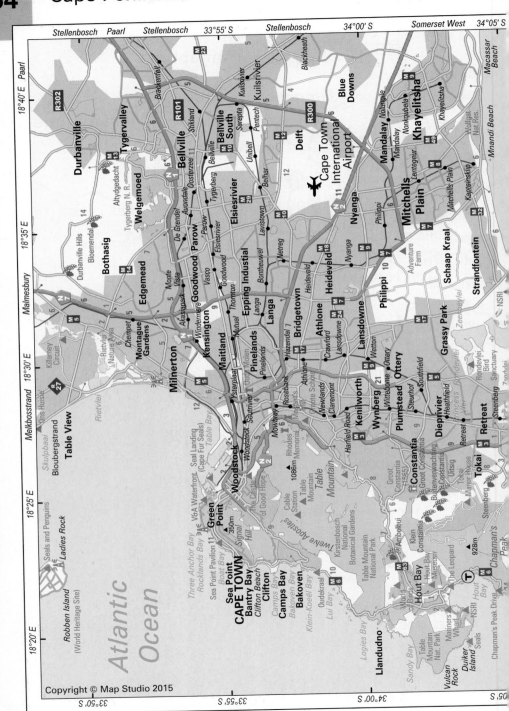

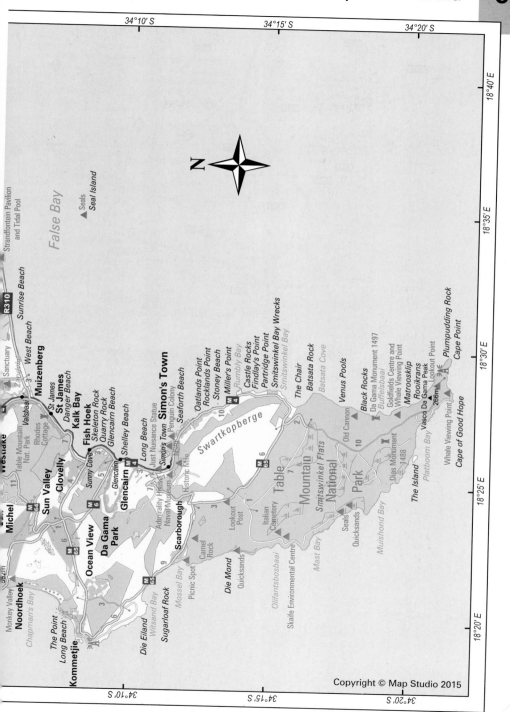

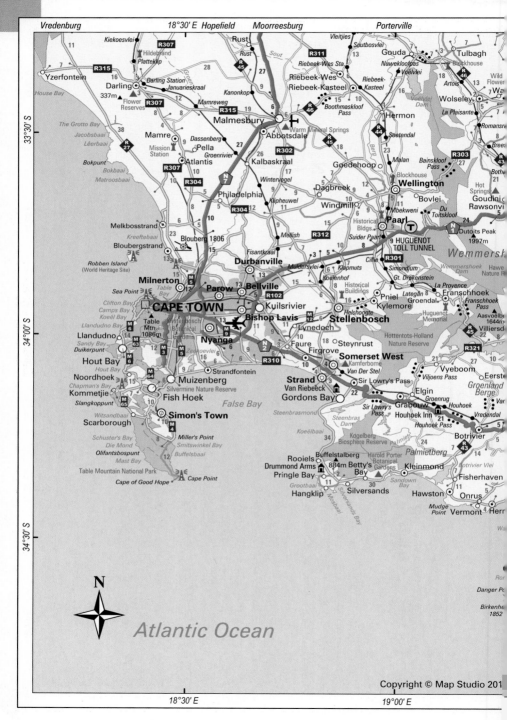

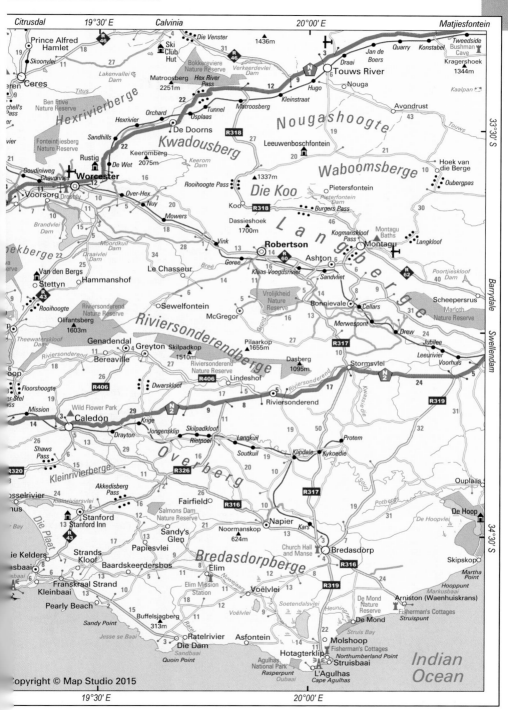

0   10   20   30   40km

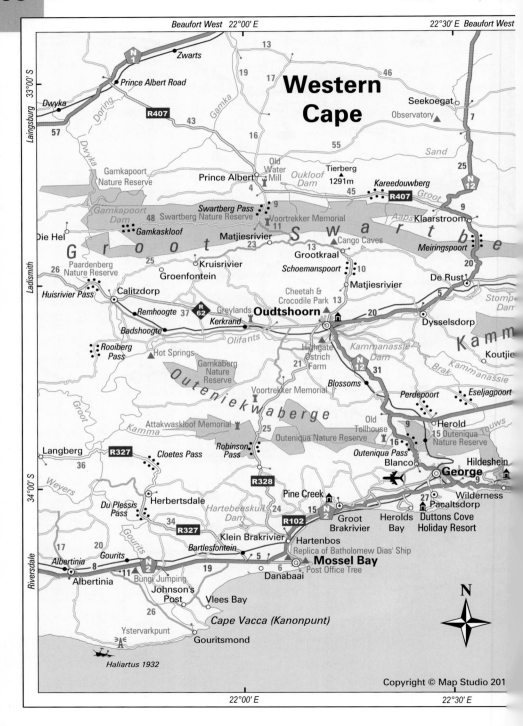

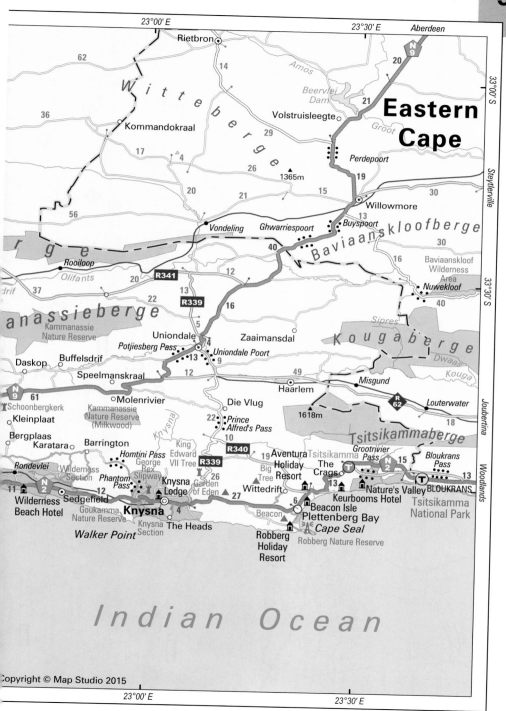

10   20   30   40km

23°00' E   23°30' E   Aberdeen

Rietbron

62   14
                                        Amos

36   Beervlei
                                        Dam   21   **Eastern**
        Kommandokraal   Volstruisleegte   **Cape**
                           29   Groot
    17   4   Perdepoort
                        26   19
        20   1365m
                    21   15   30
    56
                                            Willowmore
        Vondeling   Ghwarriespoort   Buyspoort   13   Baviaanskloofberge
    r g e   40   30
        Rooiloop   16   Baviaanskloof
    Olifants   20   R341   12   Wilderness
drif 37   13   Nuwekloof   Area
    anassieberge   22   R339 16   40
                        5   Kougaberge
        Kammanassie   Uniondale Zaaimansdal
        Nature Reserve Potjiesberg Pass   Sipres
Daskop Buffelsdrif   13 Uniondale Poort   Dwaas   Kouga
    Speelmanskraal   12   49
                        Haarlem   Misgund
    61 Schoonbergkerk   1618m   Louterwater
    Kleinplaat   Kammanassie Die Vlug   18
    Bergplaas   Nature Reserve 22 Prince   Tsitsikammaberge
    Karatara (Milkwood)   Alfred's Pass
Rondevlei   Barrington   King 10 R340 Grootrivier Bloukrans
    Wilderness Homtini Pass Edward R339 19 Aventura Tsitsikamma Pass 15 Pass
11   Section George VII Tree   Big Holiday The   13
    N2 Phantom Rex 26 Tree Resort Crags
Wilderness Sedgefield Pass Slipway Knysna Garden Wittedrift 13 Nature's Valley BLOUKRANS
Beach Hotel Goukamma Lodge of Eden 27   6 Keurbooms Hotel Tsitsikamma
    Nature Reserve **Knysna**   4 Beacon Beacon Isle National Park
Walker Point Knysna The Heads   Plettenberg Bay
        Section   Robberg Cape Seal
                    Holiday Robberg Nature Reserve
                    Resort

Indian Ocean

23°00' E   23°30' E

Scale 1 : 500 000

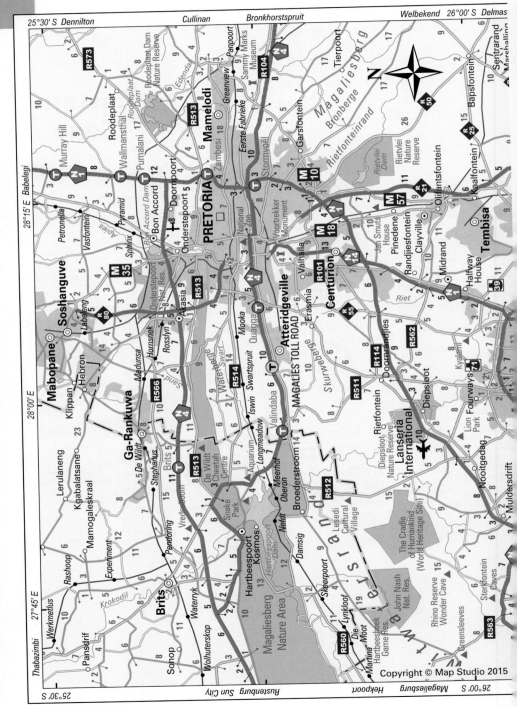

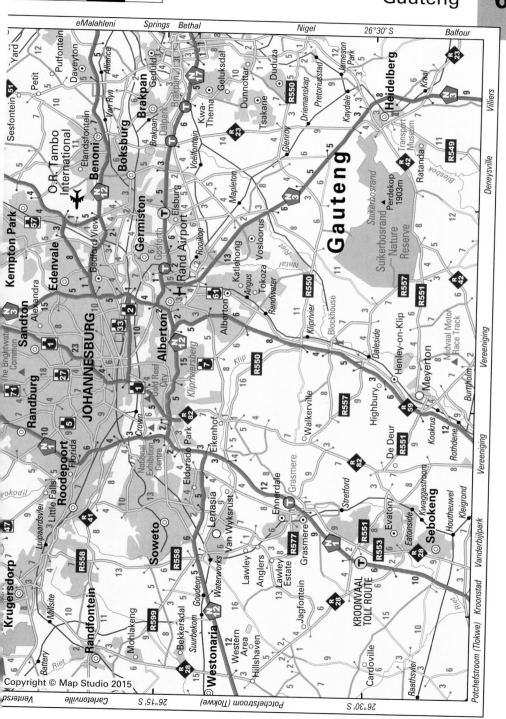

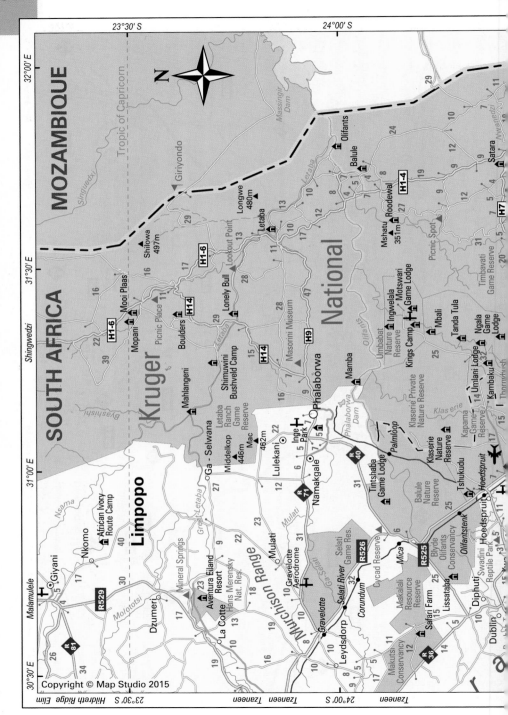

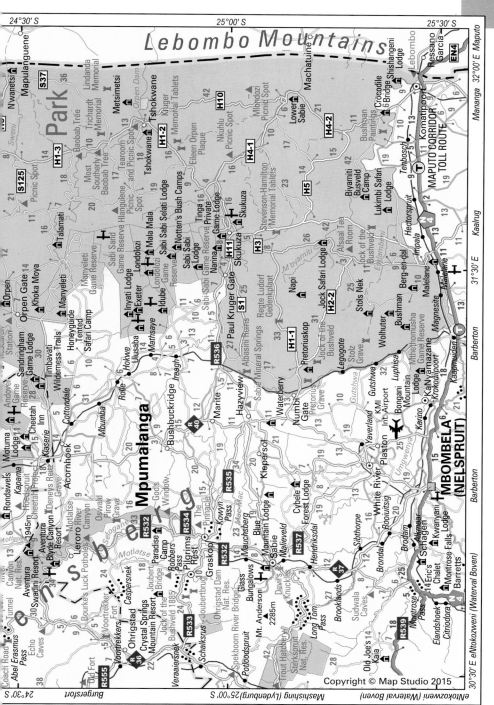

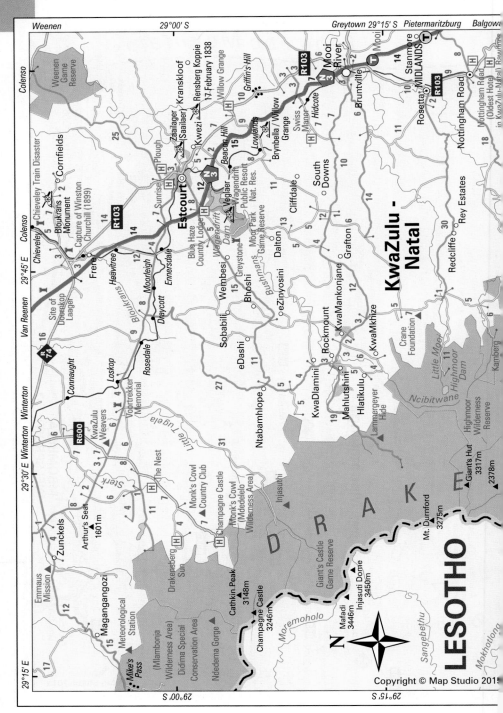

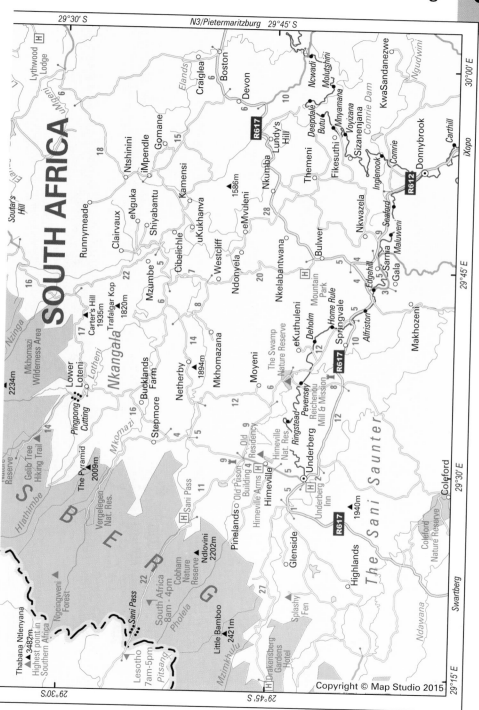

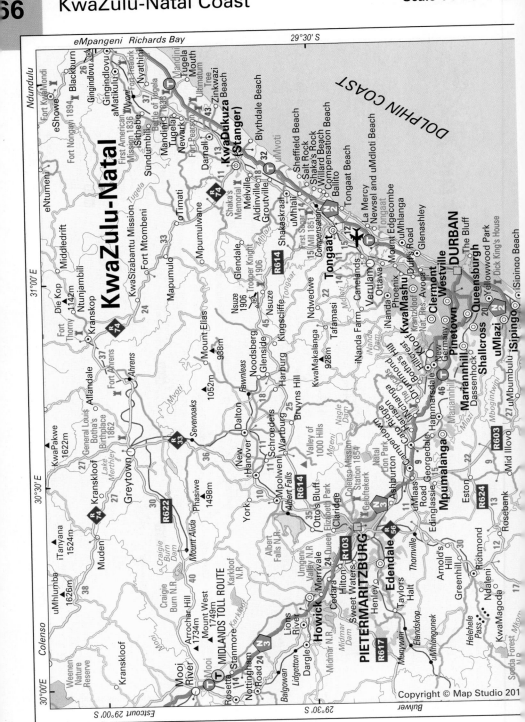

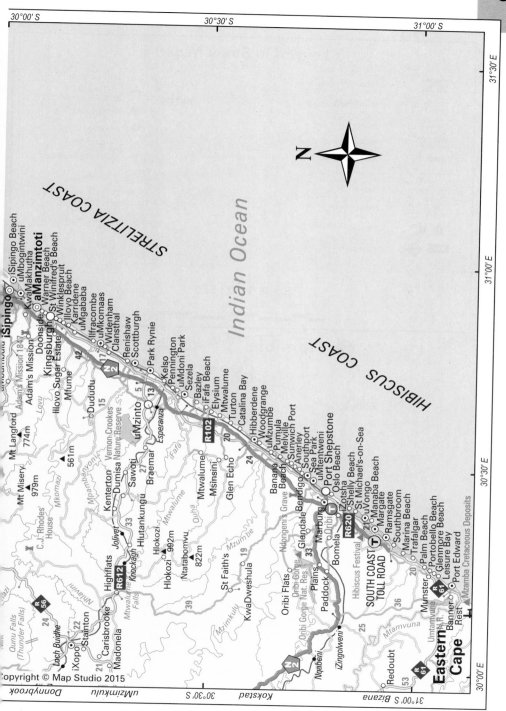

STRELITZIA COAST

HIBISCUS COAST

Indian Ocean

N

iSipingo
iSipingo Beach
uMbogintwini
KwaMakhutha
aManzimtoti
Warner Beach
Doonside
Winklespruit
St Winifred's Beach
Kingsburgh
Illovo Beach
Illovo Sugar Estate
Mfume
Karridene
uMgababa
Adam's Mission 184
Ilfracombe
uMkomaas
Widenham
Clansthal
Renishaw
Scottburgh
Park Rynie
Kelso
Pennington
uMdoni Park
Sezela
Bazley
iFafa Beach
Elysium
Mtwalume
Turton
Catalina Bay
Hibberdene
Woodgrange
uMzumbe
Pumula
Banana Beach
Melville
Sunwich Port
Bendigo
Anerley
Southport
Sea Park
uMtentweni
Port Shepstone
Oslo Beach
iZotsha
Shelly Beach
St Michael's-on-Sea
uVongo
Manaba Beach
Margate
Ramsgate
Southbroom
Marina Beach
Trafalgar
Palm Beach
Portobello Beach
Glenmore Beach
Leisure Bay
Port Edward
Munster
Mzamba Cretaceous Deposits

Mt Langford
774m
Mt Misery
979m
C.J.'Rhodes'
House
561m
Dududu
uMzinto
Vernon-Crookes
Nature Reserve
Esperanza
Mpambanyoni
Lovu
Mkomazi
Mzimkulu
Nhlavini
Mtwalume
Ifafa
Oribi
Ouha
Mzumbe
Mtamvuna
Ngabeni

Donnybrook
uMzimkulu
Koksstad
Bizana

Qunu Falls
(Thunder Falls)
Loch Bruche
iXopo
Stanton
Carisbrooke
Madonela
Highflats
Jolivet
Knockagh
Hlutankungu
Kenterton
Dumisa Nature Reserve
Sawoti
Braemar
Hlokozi
Hlokozi
Ntatabomvu
St Faith's
KwaDweshula
Oribi Flats
Oribi Gorge Nat. Res.
Oribi Gorge
Plains
Paddock
iZingolweni
Ngabeni
Redoubt
Nqobeni
Marburg
Bomela
Oribi
Hibiscus Festival
SOUTH COAST
TOLL ROAD
Ndongeni's Grave Beach
Glendale
Rest

Eastern
Cape

2
2
5
13
15
17
4
27
33
33
39
19
20
24
25
33
36
20
21
53
61
561m
992m
822m

R612
R102
R620
R56
R61

Copyright © Map Studio 2015

30°00′ S
30°30′ S
31°00′ S
30°30′ S
31°00′ S
31°30′ E
31°00′ E
30°30′ E
30°00′ E

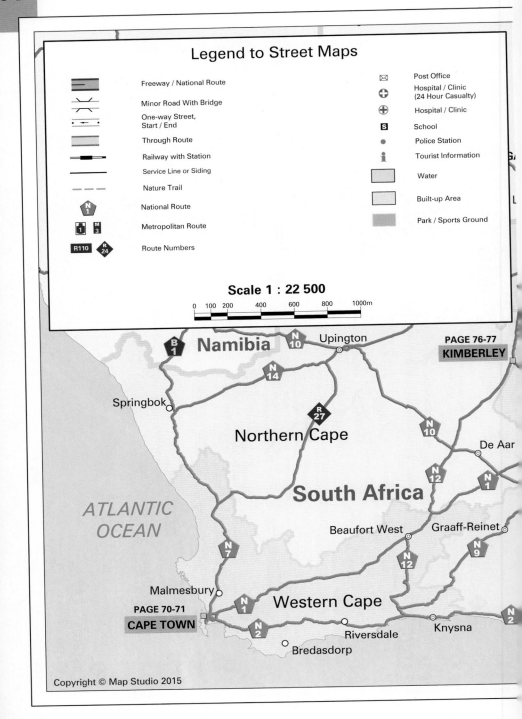

Legend to Street Maps

Freeway / National Route

Minor Road With Bridge

One-way Street,
Start / End

Through Route

Railway with Station

Service Line or Siding

Nature Trail

National Route

Metropolitan Route

Route Numbers

⊠ Post Office

✚ Hospital / Clinic
(24 Hour Casualty)

⊕ Hospital / Clinic

S School

• Police Station

i Tourist Information

Water

Built-up Area

Park / Sports Ground

Scale 1 : 22 500

0   100 200   400   600   800   1000m

Namibia   Upington

PAGE 76-77
KIMBERLEY

Springbok

Northern Cape

De Aar

South Africa

ATLANTIC
OCEAN

Beaufort West   Graaff-Reinet

Malmesbury

PAGE 70-71
CAPE TOWN

Western Cape

Riversdale   Knysna

Bredasdorp

Copyright © Map Studio 2015

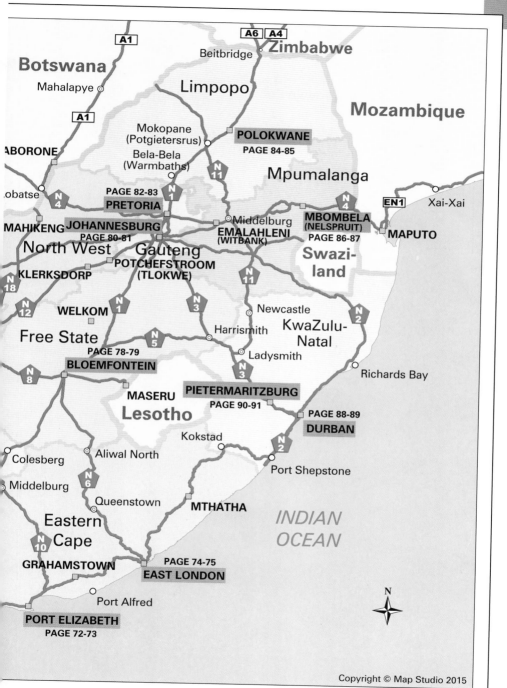

18°23'30"E   18°24'00"E   18°24'30"E

33°54'00"S
33°54'30"S
33°55'00"S
33°55'30"S
33°56'00"S

CPUT
(Granger Bay Campus)

Green Point

BEACH RD
Surrey Pl.
Rothesay Pl.
Bay Rd
Stephan Way

Mouille Point

Park Rd
Bay Rd
Alexander

CAPE TOWN
STADIUM
Green Point

Vlei Rd
Fritz Sonnenberg Rd

Three Anchor Bay
Sea Point
Stanley Pl.
Bill Peters Dr.

Three Anchor Bay
Rocklands Bay
Rocklands Beach

M6
HELEN SUZMAN BLVD
M61
MAIN RD

BEACH RD
Penarth
Fort Rd
Marine Rd
Hofmeyr Rd
Grimalay Rd
Mutley Rd
Ellerton P
Antrim Rd
Glengariff
Avondale

Richmond Rd
Bowlers Way
Hill Rd
Scholtz Rd
Leicester Rd
Croxteth
Sydney St
Dysart Rd
Torbay Rd
Haytor Rd

Rocklands Rd 1
St James Rd
Stone
Sea Point H
Norfolk Rd
Wisbeach Rd
Hall Rd

St George's Rd
St John's Rd
Braeside
Maydon
Law
Walter
Romney Rd
Sollum Rd
Cheviot Pl.
Modena

HIGH LEVEL RD
Thornhill Rd
Reddam House

London Rd
Rhine Rd
Blackheath Rd
Sea Point P
Battery Cr.

Kort
Kelvin Rd
Joubert Rd
Ocean View Dr.
Ben Nevis Rd
Roos Rd

Marais Rd
Oliver Rd
Milton Rd
Graham Rd
Lincoln Rd
Ellis Rd

MAIN RD
Conifer Rd
Albany Rd
Bellevue Rd
Bergan

Upper Main Rd
Antwerp Rd
Ocean View Dr.
Upper Rhine Rd
Ilkley Rd
Calais Rd
Dover Rd

Springbok Rd
Chepstow Rd
Ocean View Dr.
Skye Way
Carreg Cr.
Merriman Rd

Worcester Rd
Arthur's Rd
Sea Point
Tafelberg
Training Centre
The Glen
Heathfield

BEACH RD
HIGH LEVEL RD

Signal Hill
350.3m

Schotsche
Kloof

Trafalgar
Inez Rd
Duncan Rd
Arthur's Rd
Liison
Barkly Rd

1 Frere Rd
2 Rosedene Rd
3 Winstonia Rd
4 Herbert Rd

Lion's Rump

St John's Rd
Irwinton Rd
Gorleston Rd
Algakirk Rd

Ocean View Dr.

Voortrog Rd
Yusuf Dr.
Astana St
Tanabaq
Pentz St
Upper Boem St
Military Rd

Chateau
Ave St Charles
Ave De Bordeaux
Ave Fontainebleau

Vista H
St Paul's R

Protea Ave
Ave Normandie
L'Hermite
Ave Drelingcourt

Whitford St
Carsford St

Signal Hill Rd

Ave St
Charles
Ave St
Bartholomew
Ave De Berrange
Ave Disandt

Leeukloof Dr.
Devonport Rd
Kenmore Rd
Poyser Rd
Brownlow
Queens Rd
Hillside Rd
Milner Rd
Military Rd

Bennington Rd

UPPER BUITENGRACHT
NEW CHURCH ST
PARK RD
RHEE
BU
BUI

Ocean View Dr.
Ave Fresnaye
Ave Deauville
Fresnaye
Head Rd

Woodside Rd
Burnside Rd
Gilmour Rd
Belle Ombre
Warren St
Carstens St
Brunswick

Hildene Rd
Albert Rd
Bond St

Byron St
Tamboerskloof Rd

Varsity
Col.

Tamboerskloof

Deutsche Schule
Cape Town S

Upper Albert Rd
Ruel St
Bay View St
St Michael's Rd
Camden St
Hastings St
Eaton Rd
Upper Union St

L Jan van
Riebeeck
H Jan van
Riebeeck

KLOOF NEK RD
De Lorentz St
Nicol St
Welwenveden St

Cambridge
Ave
De Hoop
Ave
Varsity St
Regent Circus
Leeukop St
Kelvin St

KLOOF ST

Quarry Hill Rd
Leeuwendal

Reservoir

Camps Bay 18°24'30"E

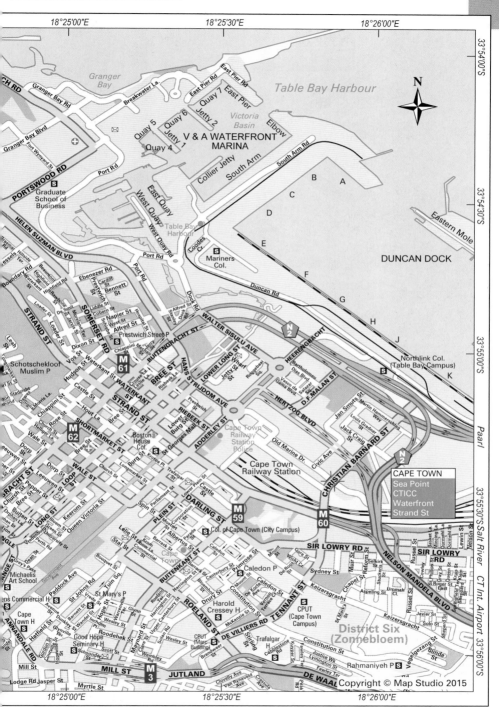

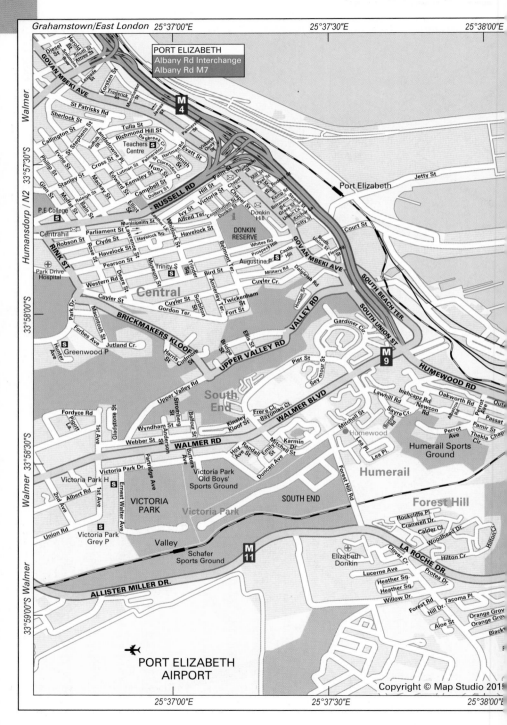

PORT ELIZABETH
Albany Rd Interchange
Albany Rd M7

PORT ELIZABETH
AIRPORT

0   500   1 000m

25°38'30"E   25°39'00"E   25°39'30"E

N

Charl Malan
Quay

33°57'30"S

33°58'00"S

Humewood
Road

M4

a Pl.
mmern St
ave

HUMEWOOD EAST

Windermere Rd

BEACH RD

Killarney Rd St
Boet St
Cyprus
Ave

Ocean Ave

Humewood Rd

Dundalk Rd
Ayliff St
Strand
Ave
Spray
View Ave

Ferndale
Rd

Mansions
Ave

McArthur

Marshall Rd

Aberdour
Cr.

33°58'30"S

Glengarry Cr.

Napier Rd

Chalmers Rd

Glengarry Cr.

Humewood

Keswick
Pl.

Glengarry Cr.

Schater Rd.

LA ROCHE DR.

M11

Cathcart Rd

Happy
Valley Dr

Humewood Beach

Brookes Hill Dr.

MARINE DR.

Lodge
Rd

M4

Schoenmakerskop 33°59'00"S

LA ROCHE DR.

STRANDFONTEIN RD

Boet Erasmus
(EPRFU)
(Telkom Park)

HAPPY VALLEY

Lodge Rd

a Ave

a P

Driftsand

Summerstrand

Caulfield Cr.

Caulfield
Cr.

Mellwraith St

Solomon St

Bloe St

Erasmus Dr.

Teachers' Training
College
Sports Ground

2nd Ave

i

25°38'30"E   *Summerstrand*   25°39'00"E   25°39'30"E

Scale 1 : 22 500

Nahoon Nahoon 33°00'00"S 33°00'30"S

Bunker's Hill Sports Field

Bunker's Hill

Sandwich Rd

Baysville

Buffalo Park Cricket Grounds

Buffalo Park Rd

EAST BANK

Old Selbornian Club

H Grens Afrikaanse

Berea

Berea Gardens

Hudson Park H

HTS Port Rex

1 Quartzite Dr.
2 Weaver Ter.

VALLEY RD

COMMERCIAL RD

Arcadia

ABSA Stadium (Basil Kenyon)

JAN SMUTS GROUND

Southernwood

St Marks Hospital

St Dominic's Hospital

Victoria Park

Belgravia

Selborne

East London Tech. Col.

Milner, Lennox Estate & Panmure

OXFORD ST

UNION AVE

LUKIN RD

ST PETERS ST

NORTH WEST EXPRESSWAY

OLD JOHN ST

Arcadia Spec.

Duncan Village

Amalinda

32°59'30"S 33°00'00"S 33°00'30"S

King William's Town/Grahamstown/N2

Mthatha/Queenstown

27°55'30"E 27°55'00"E 27°54'30"E

JOHN BAILIE RD

GALWAY RD

BEACH RD

Copyright © Map Studio 2015

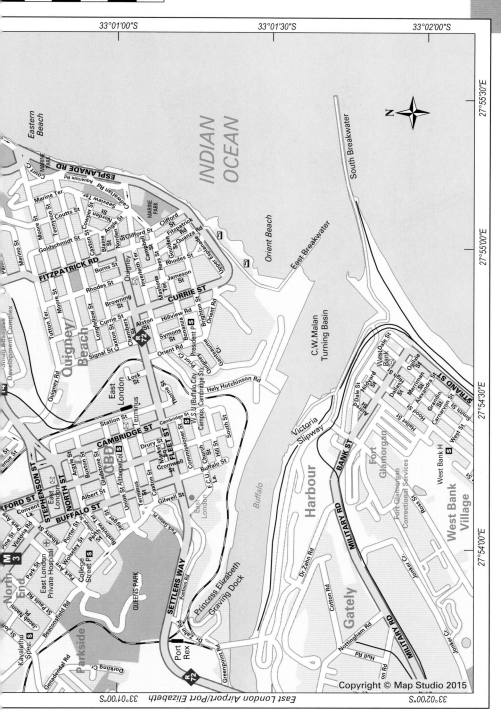

500   1 000m

33°01'00"S   33°01'30"S   33°02'00"S

27°55'30"E

27°55'00"E

27°54'30"E

27°54'00"E

INDIAN OCEAN

Eastern Beach

MARINE PARK

ESPLANADE RD

Orient Beach

East Breakwater

South Breakwater

C.W. Malan Turning Basin

FITZPATRICK RD

Quigney Beach

CURRIE ST

East London Terminus

Station St

CAMBRIDGE ST

CBD

FLEET ST

STEPHENSON ST

BUFFALO ST

KFORD ST

NORTH ST

QUEENS PARK

SETTLERS WAY

Princess Elizabeth Graving Dock

Buffalo

Victoria Slipway

Harbour

BANK ST

MILITARY RD

Fort Glamorgan

Fort Glamorgan Correctional Services

West Bank Village

West Bank H

STRAND ST

Gately

North End

M 3

Parkside

R 72

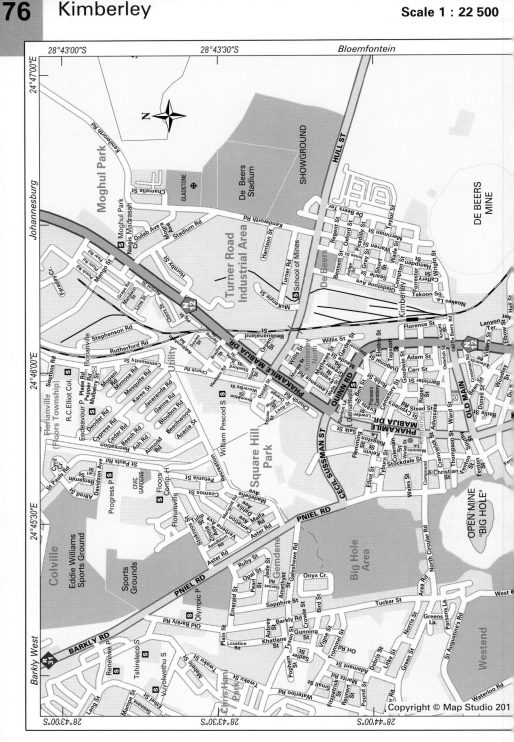

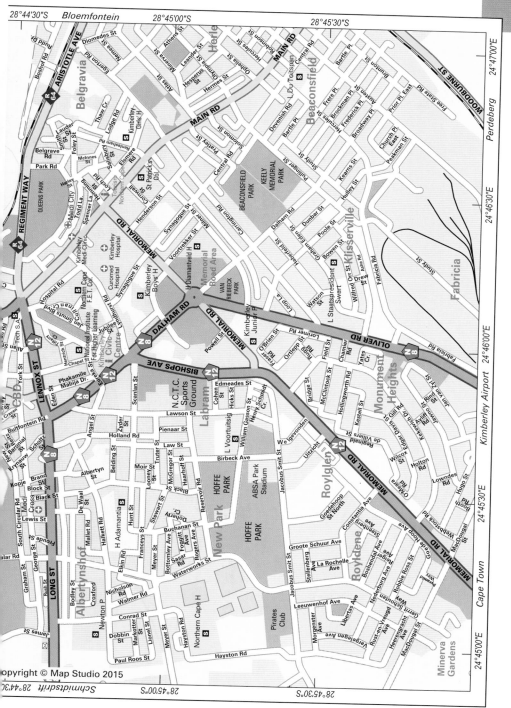

Scale 1 : 22 500

29°05'30"S 29°06'00"S 29°06'30"S *Brandfort* 29°07'00"

Bultfontein

26°13'30"E
26°13'00"E
26°12'30"E
26°12'00"E

Rayton/Hillsboro

MILNER RD

Browne St
Peter Cr.
Stewart Cr.
Fischer St
Dalville Dr.
Louis Botha St
Pade St
Goodale St
Kestell St
Whites Rd
Unie Ave
Mewan
Deane Ave
Prophet St
Paul Roux St
Kidger St
Lady Smith St
Albrecht St
Harry Smith St
Baton St
Papendis Pl
High St
Komman dant Senekal St
Goodman St
Capt. Dawson St
General van Schoor St
Plettenberg St
Klopper St
General
Van der Stel St
Jan van Riebeeck St
Borkenhagen Cr
Brebner Rd
Athlone Ave
Reyser St
Brebner Rd
Brill St
2nd Ave
Connor Ave
Bompart St
General Hertzog St
Thomson Cr.
Thomson St
Chris Botha St
Heimburger Cr.
President Steyn Ave
Reid St
Reid St
Kelher St
Reid St
Kelher Ave
President Reitz Ave
Arboretum Ave
1st Ave
Arboretum Ave
Collins Rd
Barnes St
Markgraaf St
De Villiers St
Henry St
Henry St
Elizabeth St
Charles St
Raaf St
Jock Melring St
Murray Ave
Jock Melring St
Sir George Grey Ave
Eunice P
Budd St
Kings Way
Loch Logan
KINGSPARK ZOOLOGICAL GARDENS
STAATSPRESIDENT SWART PARK
Grey Col. S

Grant's Hill
1499m

Signal Hill
1474.7m

Naval Hill
49
1499m
Reservoir

Waverley

Arboretum

Westdene

Dan Pienaar

Brandwag

Tempe Sports Club

Reservoir

R700
UNIE AVE
ALIWAL ST
HAMILTON PARK WEST
S Meisieskool Oranje
P Meisieskool Oranje
C & N
C & N
6th St
7th St
6th St
5th St
4th St
3rd St
2nd St
KLOOF ST
VAL ST
ND ST
NELSON MANDELA DR.
ZASTRON ST
W BURGER ST
E BURGER ST
ALEXANDRA AVE
RAYMOND NHLAPATST
M 30
Noordeind Rd
Bloemhof St
Cronwright St
Levy St
Lombard St
Koller St
Kruger St
Glen Signal Rd
Long St
President Kruger Ave
Bree St
JOUBERT PARK
Fairview St
Short St
Hill St
Cricket St
Fichardt St
Henry St
Fawkes Rd
Link Rd
Link St
Ramblers Club
Greyuniversity St
De Villiers St

N8
N8

HENRY ST
ZASTRON ST
GEN. DAN PIENAAR DR.

Westdene Tennis Club
3rd Ave
2nd Ave
Bloemfontein Medi-Clinic
St Andrews PS

M 19

Leviseur St
James Scott St
John Weston St
Capt. Proctal St
Captain Proctor St
Nettertop St
Kierck St
Kierck Ave
St Michael's PS
Melville Ave
Wannenberg St
Stapelberg St
Odendaal St
John Chard St
Poole St
McHardy St
Durant St
L Brandwag
Leisegang St
De Kock St
Prins St
J.D. Potgieter St
Brink St
Pappa Brits Rd
Jock
W. Hammond Rd
Dirk van Deventer St
Furstenburg Rd

Drakensberg Cr
Crisp Rd
3rd Ave PS

R 48
M 19

N

29°05'30"S 29°06'00"S *N1/Kimberley* 29°07'00"S

Copyright © Map Studio 2015

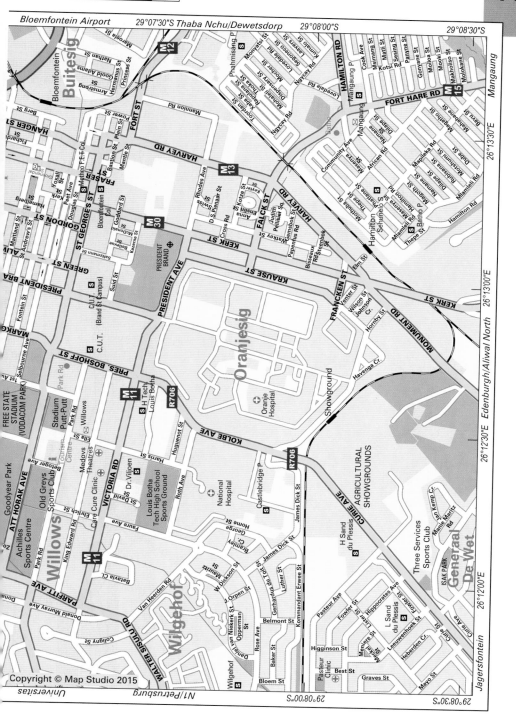

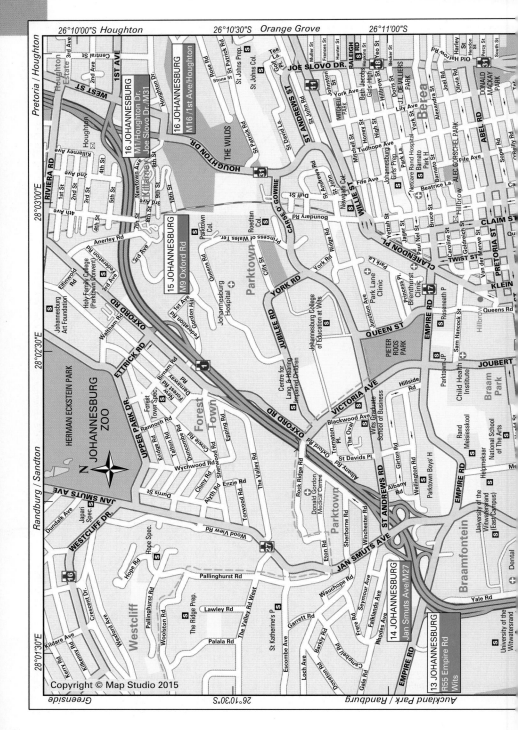

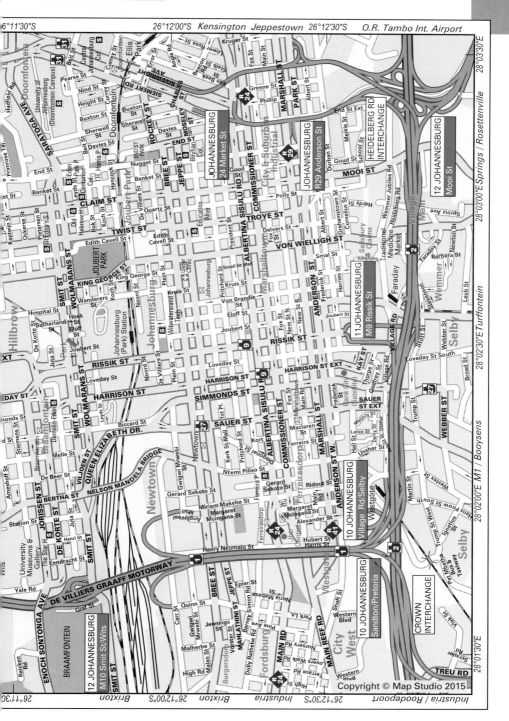

500   1 000m

26°11'30"S   26°12'00"S   Kensington Jeppestown   26°12'30"S   O.R. Tambo Int. Airport

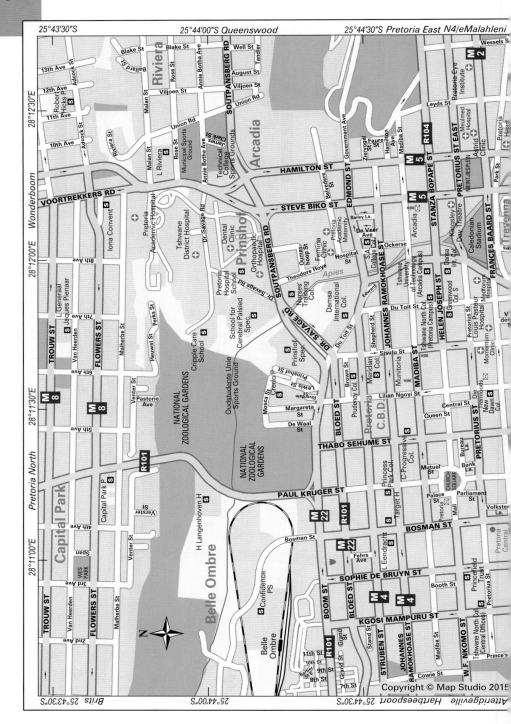

Copyright © Map Studio 2015

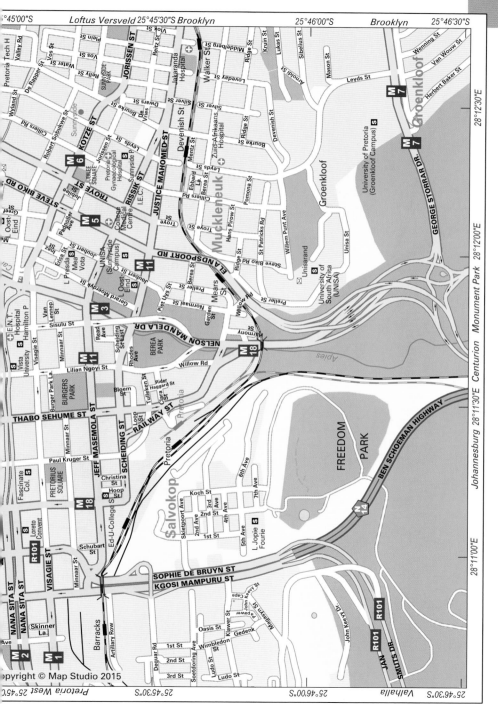

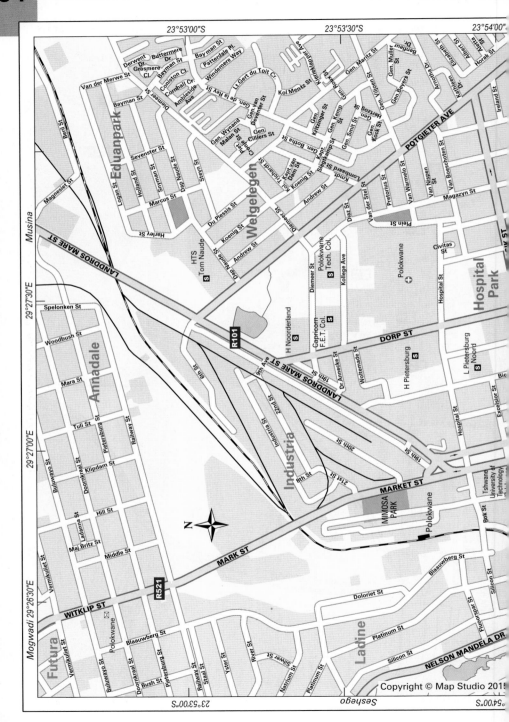

Moketsi   Tzaneen   23°54'30"S   23°55'30"S

Moregloed

Capricorn

Central Polokwane

COMPENSATIE PARK

Pietersburg Comprehensive

Polokwane English P

Limpopo Medi-Clinic

VOORTREKKER PARK

Damelin Col. (Polokwane Campus)

Danie Hough Culture Centre

LIBRARY

GARDENS

CIVIC SQUARE

Peter Mokaba Stadium

Polokwane Game Reserve

Pietersburg Club

Ivypark

Superbia

Sterkloop

POLOKWANE

Khyber Pass

Matlala   23°54'30"S   23°55'00"S   Pretoria   23°55'30"S

Copyright © Map Studio 2015

500   1 000m

23°54'30"S   23°55'30"S

29°28'00"E Polokwane Game Reserve

29°27'30"E Mashishing (Lydenburg)

29°27'00"E

29°26'30"E

25°27'30"S *Kamagugu* 25°28'00"S *Komatipoort / Maputo* 25°28'30"S

FRIEDENHEIM AVE

Oud Vadis St

Nelindia

Nelspruit Correctional Services

Buljon St

SUIKERRIET ST

Heyneke St

Timmerhout St

Kragbron St

Samora Machel Dr.

Tabak St

Petroleum St

Friedenheim Ave

H Nelspruit

L Nelspruit

Cameron St

HENSHALL ST

Hope St

Jones St

FERREIRA ST

Swem St

30°59'00"E

WOLFAARD ST

BOSCH ST

Curtie St

Brown St

Henshall St

Bester St

Ehlanzeni District Municipality

Ehlanzeni F.E.T. Col. (Central Office)

Carpe Diem

Nel St

NelMed

NelMed St

Kerkplein

BELL ST

SAMORA MACHEL DR.

Miedlinger St

Andersen St

Voortrekker St

Nelspruit

Paul Kruger St

Brown St

Andrew St

De Waal

Spruit St

Sirtus Cr.

Rocher St

Van Niekerk St

Rothery St

Hendr

Rood

Civic Centre

Brenda St

Van Rensbu

Rob Ferreira Hospital

30°58'30"E

MADIBA DR.

Bosch St

Christie Cr.

Silva St

Mopani Clinic

Ou Pretoria Pad

Plant Rd

Kiepersol St

Frankie St

Davies St

Loco Ave

Rivier St

Nelspruit Showgrounds

30°58'00"E

R40

MADIBA DR.

White River

Rapid St

Waterfall Ave

Stinkhout Cr.

Christie Cr.

Hartebeest St

Vintonia Ave

Vintonia

Ehlanzeni F.E.T. Col. (Nelspruit Campus)

Acacia Cr.

Breekenhout St

Tambor

Acacia

Karee St

Koralboom Ave

30°57'30"E

Crocodile

N

SAMORA MACHEL DR.

Penny Gum

Silver Oak

Nelsboom

Milkberry St

Leadwood St

Tricellia St

Marula

Silver Oak

Wild Fig

Flamboyant St

Paperbark St

Wild Pear

Yew Tree La.

Oak Ave

Honeysuckle Cr.

Birdwood

Wild Fig

Bitterbessie St

Long St

Poisonwood St

Cedarwood Circle

Silver Oak

Jacaranda Ave

Willow Tree La. Wk.

Bauhinia Ave

Jakkalsbessie St

Copyright © Map Studio 2015

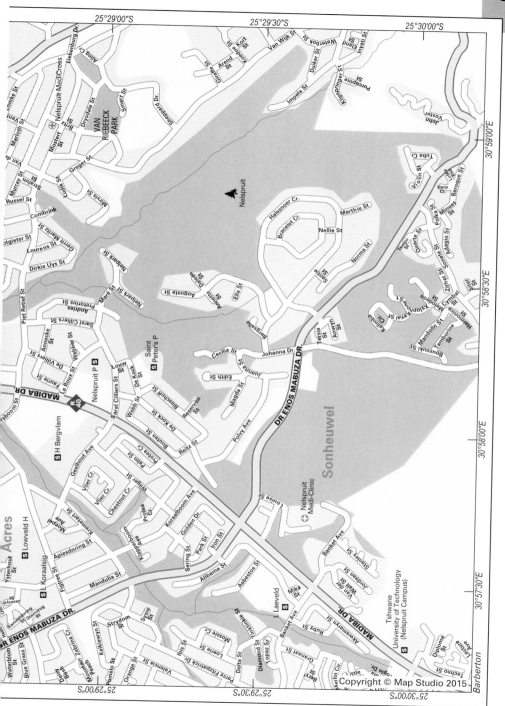

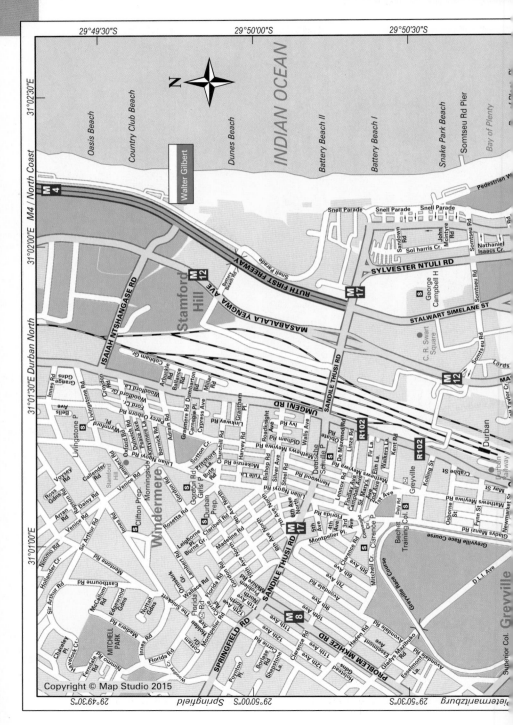

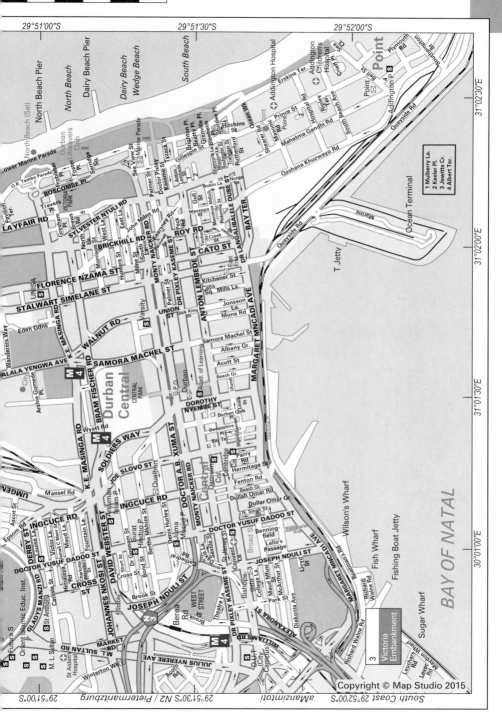

500   1 000m

29°51'00"S   29°51'30"S   29°52'00"S

North Beach Pier
Dairy Beach Pier
Dairy Beach
Wedge Beach
South Beach
North Beach
Lower North Beach (Sat)

Point

Addington Hospital
Erskine Ter.
Addington Children's Hospital
Plymouth Rd
Southampton

O.R. Tambo Parade
Foster Lifesavers Club
Seridge L
Sea View St
Prince St
Point
Masonic
Point
Hospital Rd
Ripley Ter.
South Beach Ave
Chelf Pl.
Addington P
Point Belt

BOSCOMBE PL
VICTORIA PARK
Gresham St
Brews
SYLVESTER NTULI RD
North Ridge Rd
West Ldn Rd
Palmer St
Doctor Pixley
Kaseme St
Gillespie St
Brighton Pl.
Granville Pl.
Beatty Pl.
Rutherford St
Sturdee Pl.
Hitchins St
Ocean Wk
Stearer St
Mahatma Gandhi Rd

1 Mulberry La.
2 Keeler Pl.
3 Jewitts Cr.
4 Albert Ter.

Qashana Khuzwayo Rd

LAYFAIR RD
Pavilion Per.
Travers
BRICKHILL RD
John Milne Rd
East La.
Kearsney Rd
Milne St
Hunters St
Morrison St
Robin St
Mazeppa St
Maeolive Mdedi
Creek St
Creek
Gull St
ROY RD
Pickering St
Norge
BAY TER.
DR LANGALIBALELE DUBE ST

FLORENCE NZAMA ST
MONTY NAICKER RD
Varsity
CATO ST
Kitchener St
Cato Sq.
Mills La.
ANTON LEMBEDE ST

STALWART SIMELANE ST
UNISA
Eden Gdns
WALNUT RD
K.E. MASINGA RD
UNION ST
Dick King
Palmer St
Jonsson La.
Mona Rd
MARGARET MNCADI AVE

Wanderers Way
ALALA YENGWA AVE
SAMORA MACHEL ST
Samora Machel St
Albany Gr.
Acutt St
Beach Gr.

City
Archie Gumede Pl.
BRAM FISCHER RD
Durban
Durban Central
Road of Learning
G.P.O.
Ulundi
Uhundi St

CENTRAL PARK
Wyatt Rd
DOROTHY NYEMBE ST
Durban Club
Leslie St

K.E. MASINGA RD
SOLDIERS WAY
JOE SLOVO ST
Quatbert
DR PIXLEY KASEME ST
XUMA ST
Devonshire Pl.
Bay Ter.
Parry Rd

UMGENI
Mansel Rd
Qualbert
Cambridge
Cato
Col.
Danseni
Fenton Rd
Beach Gr.
Dullah Omar Rd
Dullar Omar Gr.
T Jetty

Ascot St
INGCUCE RD
DOCTOR A.B.
MONTY NAICKER RD
Central
Anjuman
Islam
J.N. Singh St

Epsom St
DERBY ST
DAVID WEBSTER ST
Denis Hurley St
S Juma Masjid
DOCTOR YUSUF DADOO ST
Benningfield
Lello's Passage
Esplanade Ave
Wilson's Wharf

DOCTOR YUSUF DADOO RD
Victor La.
Louisa La.
Maud La.
Surat
Bertha Mkhize St
Cathedral Rd
JOSEPH NDULI ST

GLADYS MANZI RD
Carlisle St
Himalaya Rd
Charlotte
De Goomam St
Short St
Bond St
Bishops-
College La.
Park Rd
Diakonia Ave
Broad St
MARGARET MNCADI AVE

CROSS ST
JOHANNES NKOSI ST
Fountain La.
Saville St
St James St
Maud Mfusi St
McArthur St
Boermans Rd
Richard Waine Rd

St Aidan's Hospital
MARKET RD
Theatre La.
Berea Rd
Brook St
WEST STREET
DR PIXLEY KASEME ST
JOSEPH NDULI ST
WILLIAMS RD
Richard Waine Rd

M.L. Sultan Rd
JULIUS NYERERE AVE
Winterton Wlk
ALEXANDRA ST
Victoria Embankment
3

Orient Islamic Educ. Inst.
St Anthony
Futura S
M. L. Sultan

Ocean Terminal
Quayside Rd
Marine

BAY OF NATAL

Fish Wharf
Fishing Boat Jetty
Sugar Wharf
Haydon Wharf
Lever Wharf
Leuchars St

31°02'30"E   31°02'00"E   31°01'30"E   31°01'00"E   30°01'00"E   30°01'30"E   31°02'00"E

South Coast 29°52'00"S   Manzimtoti   29°51'30"S N2 / Pietermaritzburg   29°51'00"S

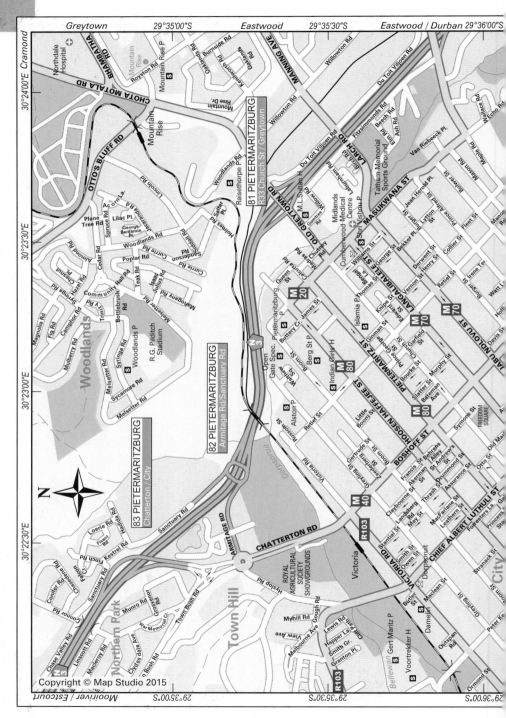

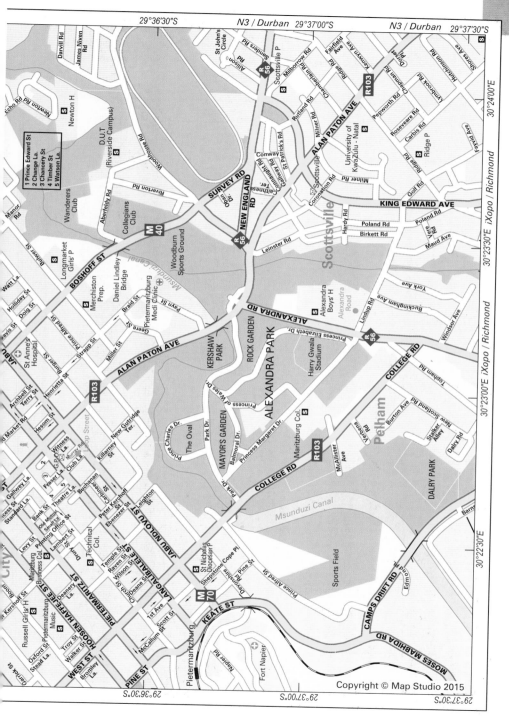

Index to Place Names

Abbreviations: E.C. - Eastern Cape Lim. - Limpopo N.W. - North West Gau. - Gauteng KZN - KwaZulu-Natal W.C. - Western Cape N.C. - Northern Cape Mpum. - Mpumalanga F.S. - Free State Zim. - Zimbabwe Moz. - Mozambique Swa. - Swaziland Les. - Lesotho Bot. - Botswana Nam. - Namibia

NAME	PG	GRID	NAME	PG	GRID	NAME	PG	GRID	NAME	PG	GRID
AALWYNSFONTEIN	21	CT 56	AVOCA	46	CJ 86	BERGRIVIER	12	CY 55	BOKSBURG	45	CK 79
AANDSTER	35	CN 72	AVONDRUST	7	DA 60	BERGSIG	23	CT 63	BOKSPITS	32	CL 61
AANSLUIT	33	CL 65	AVONTUUR	33	CL 66	BERGVILLE	37	CP 82	BOKSPUTS	23	CQ 63
ABBOTSDALE	6	DA 56				BERLIN	18	CY 78	BOLIVIA	37	CN 80
ABERDEEN	15	CX 69	BAARDSKEERDERSBOS	7	DC 58	BERMOLLI	33	CP 66	BON ACCORD	45	CJ 79
ABERDEEN ROAD	16	CY 70	BABANANGO	38	CP 86	BERSEBA	35	CM 72	BONNIEVALE	7	DB 59
ABERFELDY	37	CO 80	BABANGU	50	CD 85	BESEMPAN	35	CO 74	BONNY RIDGE	28	CT 82
ACORNHOEK	46	CF 86	BABELEGI	45	CH 79	BESTERS	38	CP 83	BONTRAND	28	CT 83
ADAMS MISSION	28	CS 85	BABERSPAN	35	CL 73	BETHAL	45	CK 82	BONZA BAY	18	CY 79
ADDO	10	DA 73	BADPLAAS	46	CJ 85	BETHANIA	26	CR 74	BOONS	44	CJ 77
ADELAIDE	17	CY 75	BADSHOOGTE	8	DA 63	BETHANIE (N.W.)	44	CH 77	BOORD	46	CJ 83
ADENDORP	16	CX 70	BAILDEN	28	CT 82	BETHANIE (NAM.)	30	CL 52	BORCHERS	50	CC 84
ADVANCE	14	CV 63	BAILEY	17	CW 75	BETHELSDORP	10	DA 72	BOSHOEK	44	CH 77
AFGUNS	48	CE 78	BAINE'S DRIFT (BOT.)	49	CV 62	BETHESDAWEG	16	CW 70	BOSHOF	35	CP 72
AFSAAL	47	CH 87	BAKENKLIP	14	CV 62	BETHLEHEM	37	CO 79	BOSKUIL	35	CM 74
AGGENEYS	21	CQ 56	BAKENSKOP	24	CQ 69	BETHULIE	26	CT 74	BOSOORD	46	CH 84
AGTER SNEEUBERG	16	CW 72	BAKERVILLE	43	CJ 74	BETTIESDAM	37	CL 82	BOSPOORT	35	CL 74
AGTERTANG	25	CU 72	BALFOUR (E.C.)	17	CY 75	BETTY'S BAY	6	DC 57	BOSSIEKOM	22	CR 59
AHRENS	28	CQ 85	BALFOUR (MPUM.)	37	CL 80	BEWLEY	43	CJ 73	BOTHASPUT	35	CP 72
AI-AIS (NAM.)	30	CO 53	BALGOWAN	28	CR 83	BEYERSBURG	23	CU 65	BOTHAVILLE (F.S.)	25	CQ 73
AKANOUS (NAM.)	40	CF 59	BALLENGEICH	38	CN 84	BHISHO	17	CY 77	BOTHAVILLE (F.S.)	36	CM 75
ALBERT FALLS	28	CR 85	BALLITO	29	CR 86	BHOLO	18	CX 78	BOTHITHONG	34	CM 68
ALBERTINIA	8	DB 63	BALTIMORE	42	CF 80	BHOLOTHWA	17	CW 76	BOTLOKWA	50	CD 83
ALBERTON	45	CK 79	BAMBOESKLOOF	26	CU 77	BHUNYA (SWA.)	38	CL 86	BOTRIVIER	6	DB 57
ALDAM	36	CO 77	BAMBOESSPRUIT	35	CL 74	BIDDULPH	36	CO 78	BOTSHABELO	26	CQ 75
ALDERLEY	18	CX 81	BANDELIERKOP	50	CD 83	BIERSPRUIT	44	CG 76	BO-WADRIF	13	CX 60
ALDINVILLE	29	CR 86	BANDUR	49	CB 82	BIESIESPOORT	15	CW 67	BOWKER'S PARK	17	CW 75
ALETTESRUS	34	CL 70	BANK	44	CK 77	BIESIESVLEI	43	CK 73	BOYNE	50	CE 83
ALEXANDER BAY	30	CP 51	BANKKOP	38	CL 84	BIG BEND (SWA.)	39	CL 88	BRAAMSPRUIT	26	CU 76
ALEXANDRIA	11	DA 75	BANNER REST	28	CU 84	BIGGARSBERG	38	CO 84	BRAEMAR	28	CT 85
ALHEIT	32	CP 60	BAPSFONTEIN	45	CJ 80	BILDEMAR	26	CT 76	BRAKBOS	23	CR 64
ALICE	17	CY 76	BARAKKE	16	CX 71	BISI	28	CT 83	BRAKFONTEIN (F.S.)	25	CR 71
ALICEDALE	17	CZ 74	BARANDAS	9	DA 64	BITTERFONTEIN	21	CU 55	BRAKFONTEIN (KZN)	38	CO 86
ALIWAL NORTH	26	CU 76	BARBERTON	46	CJ 86	BITYI	18	CW 80	BRAKFONTEIN (N.C.)	25	CS 70
ALLANRIDGE	36	CN 75	BARKLY EAST	27	CU 78	BIVANE	38	CN 85	BRAKKLOOF	17	CZ 75
ALLDAYS	49	CB 81	BARKLY PASS	18	CV 78	BIZANA	28	CU 83	BRAKPAN	45	CK 80
ALLEMAN	36	CP 75	BARKLY WEST	34	CP 70	BLACK ROCK	33	CM 66	BRAKPOORT	15	CV 67
ALLEP	25	CR 72	BARNARD	15	CV 67	BLADGROND	22	CQ 59	BRAKSPRUIT	36	CL 75
ALMA	45	CF 79	BARNEA	37	CO 79	BLAIRBETH	43	CH 74	BRAND	24	CT 69
ALPHA	38	CN 86	BARODA	16	CW 73	BLANCO	8	DB 65	BRAND PARK	35	CO 74
AMABELE	18	CY 78	BAROE	16	CZ 70	BLESKOP	44	CJ 77	BRANDBOOM	22	CU 58
AMAKHASI	38	CP 84	BARRINGTON	9	DB 66	BLESMANSPOS	34	CN 70	BRANDDRAAI	46	CF 85
AMALIA	35	CM 71	BARRYDALE	7	DA 61	BLETTERMAN	24	CU 69	BRANDFORT (F.S.)	35	CP 73
AMANZIMTOTI	29	CS 86	BARTLESFONTEIN	8	DB 64	BLINKFONTEIN	34	CN 68	BRANDFORT (F.S.)	36	CP 75
AMERSFOORT	38	CM 83	BATHURST	11	DA 76	BLINKKLIP	34	CO 67	BRANDKOP	12	CV 57
AMSTERDAM	38	CL 85	BAVIAAN	13	CZ 61	BLINKWATER (E.C.)	17	CY 75	BRANDLAAGTE	37	CP 79
ANCONA	36	CN 75	BAYALA	39	CN 89	BLINKWATER (LIM.)	49	CC 82	BRANDRIVIER	8	DA 62
ANDRIESKRAAL	10	DA 70	BAYENI	39	CO 87	BLOEMFONTEIN	26	CQ 74	BRANDVLEI	22	CT 60
ANDRIESVALE	32	CL 61	BAZLEY	28	CT 85	BLOEMHOEK	26	CT 74	BRANDWAG	26	CT 76
ANYSBERG	7	DA 61	BEACON BAY	18	CY 79	BLOEMHOF	35	CN 73	BRAUNSCHWEIG (E.C.)	17	CY 77
ANYSSPRUIT	38	CM 85	BEACONSFIELD	34	CO 68	BLOOD RIVER	38	CO 85	BRAUNSCHWEIG (MPUM.)	38	CM 85
ARCADIA	37	CO 82	BEAUFORT WEST	14	CX 65	BLOSSOMS	8	CO 86	BRAUNVILLE	17	CW 76
ARGENT	45	CK 80	BEAUTY	48	CC 78	BLOUBANK	38	CO 86	BRAY	42	CH 68
ARIAMSVLEI (NAM.)	32	CO 59	BEDFORD	17	CY 74	BLOUBERG	49	CC 81	BREAKFAST VLEI	17	CZ 76
ARIESFONTEIN	34	CO 68	BEDFORD	17	CY 74	BLOUBERGSTRAND	6	DA 55	BREDASDORP	7	DC 60
ARLINGTON	36	CO 78	BEERLEY	26	CU 76	BLOUHAAK	49	CC 82	BREIDBACH	17	CY 77
ARNISTON (WAENHUISKRANS)	7	DC 60	BEESHOEK	33	CO 66	BLOUSYFER	13	CV 61	BREIPAAL	26	CS 74
AROAB (NAM.)	31	CL 58	BEESTEKRAAL	44	CH 78	BLUECLIFF	10	DA 72	BREYTEN	46	CK 84
ARUNDEL	25	CU 71	BEHULPSAAM	16	CX 71	BLUEGUMS	26	CT 73	BRIDGEWATER	49	CB 81
ASBOSPAN (NAM.)	30	CL 51	BEITBRIDGE	50	CA 83	BLUEWATER BAY	10	DA 73	BRITS	44	CJ 78
ASHBURTON	28	CR 84	BEKKER	34	CN 68	BLYDSKAP	37	CN 80	BRITSTOWN	24	CT 68
ASHTON	7	DA 59	BELA VISTA (MOZ.)	47	CK 90	BOANE (MOZ.)	47	CK 89	BRITTEN	35	CN 72
ASKEATON	17	CW 77	BELA-BELA (WARMBATHS)	45	CG 79	BOBONONG (BOT.)	49	CA 79	BROEDERSPUT	35	CL 71
ASKHAM	32	CM 61	BELFAST (EMAKHAZENI)	46	CJ 83	BOCHUM (SENWABARANA)	49	CC 81	BROKEN DAM	24	CT 67
ASKRAAL	7	DB 61	BELGRAVIA	13	CW 61	BODAM	22	CU 60	BROMBEEK	49	CB 82
ASSEGAAIBOS	10	DB 70	BELL	17	CZ 77	BODENSTEIN	44	CK 75	BRONDAL	46	CH 86
ASSEN	44	CH 78	BELLEVUE (E.C.)	17	CZ 74	BOEGOEBERG	23	CQ 65	BRONKHORSTSPRUIT	45	CJ 81
ASTON BAY	10	DB 71	BELLEVUE (LIM.)	49	CC 82	BOERBOONFONTEIN	7	DA 60	BROOKS NEK	28	CT 82
ATLANTA	44	CH 78	BELLVILLE	6	DA 56	BOESMANSKOP	26	CS 77	BRUGHALTE	26	CT 76
ATLANTIS	6	DA 55	BELMONT	25	CR 70	BOESMANSRIVIERMOND	11	DA 76	BRUINTJIESHOOGTE	16	CY 72
ATTERIDGEVILLE	45	CJ 79	BENONI	45	CK 80	BOETSAP	34	CO 70	BUCHHOLZBRUNN (NAM.)	30	CL 52
AUGRABIES	32	CP 60	BERBICE	38	CM 86	BOHLOKONG	37	CO 79	BUCKLANDS	24	CQ 68
AURORA	12	CY 56	BEREAVILLE	7	DB 58	BOKHARA	32	CO 60	BUFFELSDRIF	9	DA 66
AUSTIN'S POST	25	CR 73	BERGPLAAS	9	DA 64	BOKKOPPIE	34	CO 67	BUFFELSKLIP	9	DA 66
						BOKNES	11	DA 75			

Index to Place Names

Index to Place Names

NUMBER	COORDINATES	PG	GRID
1	33°53'06.89"S 18°31'52.92"E	6	DA 56
2	34°13'38.67"S 19°25'44.69"E	7	DB 58
3	34°05'16.94"S 20°05'26.17"E	7	DB 60
4	34°05'37.02"S 21°15'04.27"E	8	DB 62
5	33°59'07.37"S 22°30'32.68"E	8	DB 65
6	33°49'09.52"S 22°21'16.45"E	8	DA 65
7	33°01'31.16"S 18°06'24.59"E	12	CZ 55
8	32°21'50.38"S 18°56'21.46"E	12	CX 57
9	32°10'23.26"S 18°52'03.59"E	12	CX 56
10	33°13'28.34"S 20°34'54.32"E	13	CZ 61
11	32°22'35.01"S 22°31'37.07"E	14	CX 65
12	31°53'04.81"S 23°05'00.19"E	15	CW 67
13	32°15'00.39"S 24°32'07.63"E	16	CX 70
14	31°29'49.21"S 25°00'19.78"E	16	CV 71
15	33°36'43.84"S 25°54'49.89"E	11	DA 74
16	32°57'49.68"S 27°55'11.63"E	18	CY 78
17	32°00'23.03"S 27°00'15.07"E	17	CW 76
18	30°41'36.58"S 26°42'31.92"E	26	CU 75
19	31°35'18.03"S 28°47'24.22"E	18	CW 81
20	30°45'10.01"S 30°25'58.31"E	28	CU 84
21	29°50'26.62"S 30°57'26.06"E	29	CS 86
22	29°13'26.69"S 30°00'17.67"E	28	CQ 84
23	28°35'15.69"S 29°36'32.13"E	38	CP 83
24	28°00'44.37"S 32°14'18.03"E	39	CO 89
25	27°02'27.02"S 30°48'48.83"E	38	CM 85
26	26°08'55.77"S 30°46'15.05"E	46	CK 85
27	26°31'17.01"S 29°59'07.76"E	38	CL 83
28	26°27'11.36"S 29°27'57.69"E	45	CK 82
29	25°53'35.96"S 29°15'42.85"E	45	CJ 82
30	25°49'46.36"S 29°31'43.29"E	45	CJ 82
31	25°27'03.12"S 30°42'35.02"E	46	CH 85
32	23°04'41.75"S 29°54'31.18"E	50	CC 83
33	23°16'03.03"S 28°26'12.96"E	49	CD 80
34	24°17'13.52"S 28°58'54.82"E	45	CF 81
35	24°55'08.66"S 28°22'22.19"E	45	CG 79
36	25°38'45.65"S 28°16'29.69"E	45	CJ 79
37	26°02'34.05"S 28°06'08.13"E	45	CJ 79
38	26°15'49.06"S 27°57'24.24"E	44	CK 78
39	25°43'46.12"S 27°39'57.36"E	44	CJ 78
40	25°32'42.08"S 26°04'44.54"E	43	CH 74
41	26°20'29.92"S 26°18'18.33"E	43	CK 74
42	25°51'48.64"S 25°38'46.56"E	43	CJ 73
43	26°57'31.42"S 24°43'56.14"E	35	CM 71
44	27°39'24.78"S 27°14'59.54"E	36	CN 77
45	28°29'56.73"S 26°59'52.09"E	36	CP 76
46	27°19'24.26"S 28°46'36.22"E	37	CM 80
47	28°17'16.19"S 29°08'01.49"E	37	CO 81
48	29°17'51.19"S 27°27'08.88"E	26	CQ 77
49	29°12'05.37"S 26°11'27.63"E	26	CQ 74
50	28°44'56.14"S 24°45'56.08"E	35	CP 71
51	28°06'46.15"S 24°51'12.63"E	35	CO 71
52	27°53'55.73"S 22°57'45.61"E	33	CO 66
53	28°27'36.77"S 21°14'26.97"E	32	CP 62
54	29°07'30.62"S 19°23'55.76"E	22	CQ 58
55	29°39'41.58"S 17°53'33.64"E	21	CR 54
56	29°41'23.27"S 22°44'26.84"E	24	CR 66
57	30°34'44.76"S 23°30'37.07"E	24	CT 68
58	31°04'32.28"S 24°25'55.92"E	25	CU 70
59	30°43'59.36"S 25°05'05.63"E	25	CU 72